Mechanical Drawing Self-Taught:

by
Joshua Rose

COMPRISING

INSTRUCTIONS IN THE SELECTION AND
PREPARATION OF DRAWING INSTRUMENTS,

*ELEMENTARY INSTRUCTION IN PRACTICAL
MECHANICAL DRAWING*;

TOGETHER WITH

EXAMPLES IN SIMPLE GEOMETRY AND ELEMENTARY
MECHANISM, INCLUDING SCREW THREADS, GEAR
WHEELS, MECHANICAL MOTIONS, ENGINES AND
BOILERS.

AUTHOR OF "THE COMPLETE PRACTICAL
MACHINIST," "THE PATTERN MAKER'S ASSISTANT,"
"THE SLIDE VALVE"

ILLUSTRATED BY THREE HUNDRED AND THIRTY
ENGRAVINGS.

PREFACE.

The object of this book is to enable the beginner to learn to make simple mechanical drawings without the aid of an instructor, and to create an interest in the subject by giving examples such as the machinist meets with in his every-day workshop practice. The plan of representing in many examples the pencil lines, and numbering the order in which they are marked, the author believes to possess great advantages for the learner, since it is the producing of the pencil lines that really proves the study, the inking in being merely a curtailed repetition of the pencilling. Similarly when the drawing of a piece, such, for example, as a fully developed screw thread, is shown fully developed from end to end, even though the pencil lines were all shown, yet the process of construction will be less clear than if the process of development be shown gradually along the drawing. Thus beginning at an end of the example the first pencil lines only may be shown, and as the pencilling progresses to the right-hand, the development may progress so that at the other or left-hand end, the finished inked in and shaded thread may be shown, and between these two ends will be found a part showing each stage of development of the thread, all the lines being numbered in the order in which they were marked. This prevents a confusion of lines, and makes it more easy to follow or to copy the drawing.

It is the numerous inquiries from working machinists for a book of this kind that have led the author to its production, which he hopes and believes will meet the want thus indicated, giving to the learner a sufficiently practical knowledge of mechanical drawing to enable him to proceed further by copying such drawings as he may be able to obtain, or by the aid of some of the more expensive and elaborate books already published on the subject.

He believes that in learning mechanical drawing without the aid of an instructor the chief difficulty is overcome when the learner has become sufficiently familiar with the instruments to be enabled to use them without hesitation or difficulty, and it is to attain this end that the chapter on plotting mechanical motions and the succeeding examples have been introduced; these forming studies that are easily followed by the beginner; while sufficiently interesting to afford to the student pleasure as well as profit.

New York, *February, 1883.*

CONTENTS.

end that the chapter on plotting mechanical motions and the succeeding examples have been introduced; these forming studies that are easily followed by the beginner; while sufficiently interesting to afford to the student pleasure as well as profit.

New York, *February, 1883.*

CONTENTS.

CHAPTER I.

THE DRAWING BOARD.

A Drawing Board should be of soft pine and free from knots, so that it will easily receive the pins or tacks used to fasten down the paper. Its surface should be flat and level, or a little rounding, so that the paper shall lie close to its surface, which is one of the first requisites requisites in making a good drawing. Its edges should be straight and at a right angle one to the other, and the ends of the battens B B in Figure 1should fall a little short of the edge A of the board, so that if the latter shrinks they will not protrude. The size of the board of course depends upon the size of the paper, hence it is best to obtain a board as small as will answer for the size of paper it is intended to use. The student will find it most convenient as well as cheapest to learn on small drawings rather than large ones, since they take less time to make, and cost less for paper; and although they require more skill to make, yet are preferable for the beginner, because he does not require to reach so far over the board, and furthermore, they teach him more quickly and effectively. He who can make a fair drawing having short lines and small curves can make a better one if it has large curves, etc., because it is easier to draw a large than a very small circle or curve. It is unnecessary to enter into a description of the various kinds of drawing boards in use, because if the student purchases one he will be duly informed of the kinds and their special features, while if he intends to make one the sketch in Figure 1 will give him all the information he requires, save that, as before noted, the wood must be soft pine, well seasoned and free from knots, while the battens B should be dovetailed in and the face of the board trued after they are glued and driven in. To true the edges square, it is best to make the two longest edges parallel and straight, and then the ends may be squared from those long edges.

Fig. 1.

THE T SQUARE.

Drawing squares or T squares, as they are termed, are made of wood, of hard rubber and of steel.

There are several kinds of T squares; in one the blade is solid, as it is shown in Figure 5 on page 20; in another the back of the square is pivoted, so that the blade can be set to draw lines at an angle as well as across the board, which is often very convenient, although this double back prevents the triangles, when used in some positions, from coming close enough to the left hand side of the board. In an improved form of steel square, with pivoted blade, shown in Figure 2, the back is provided with a half circle divided into the degrees of a circle, so that the blade can be set to any required degree of angle at once.

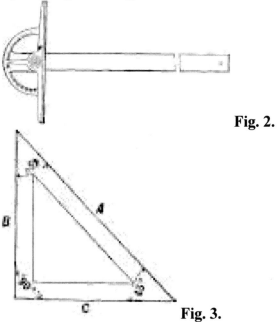

Fig. 2.

Fig. 3.

Fig. 4.

THE TRIANGLES.

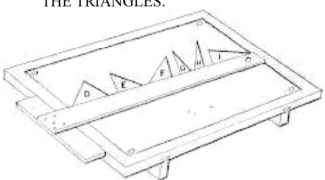

Fig. 5.

Two triangles are all that are absolutely necessary for a beginner. The first is that shown in Figure 3, which is called a triangle of 45 degrees, because its edge A is at that angle to edges B and C. That in Figure 4 is called a triangle of 60 degrees, its edge A being at 60 degrees to B, and at 30 degrees to C. The edges P and C are at a right angle or an angle of 90 degrees in both figures; hence they are in this respect alike. By means of these triangles alone, a great many straight line drawings may be made with ease without the use of a drawing square; but it is better for the beginner to use the square at first. The manner of using these triangles with the square is shown in Figure 5, in which the triangle, Figure 3, is shown in three positions marked D E F, and that shown in Figure 4 is shown in three positions, marked respectively G H and I. It is obvious, however, that by turning I over, end for end, another position is attained. The usefulness in these particular triangles is because in the various positions shown they are capable of use for drawing a very large proportion of the lines that occur in mechanical drawing. The principal requirement in their use is to hold them firmly to the square-blade without moving it, and without permitting them to move upon it. The learner will find that this is best attained by so regulating the height of the square-blade that the line to be drawn does not come down too near the bottom of the triangle or edge of the square-blade, nor too high on the triangle; that is to say, too near its uppermost point. It is the left-hand edge of the triangle that is used, whenever it can be done, to produce the required line.

Fig. 6.

CURVES.

To draw curves that are not formed of arcs or parts of circles, templates called curves are provided, examples of these forms being given in Figure 6. They are made in wood and in hard rubber, the latter being most durable; their uses are so obvious as to require no explanation. It may be remarked, however, that the use of curves gives excellent practice, because they must be adjusted very accurately to produce good results, and the drawing pen must be held in the same vertical plane, or the curve drawn will not be true in its outline.

DRAWING INSTRUMENTS.

It is not intended or necessary to enter into an elaborate discussion of the various kinds of drawing instruments, since the purchaser can obtain a good set of drawing instruments from a reputable dealer by paying a proportionate price, and must *per force* learn to use such as his means enable him to purchase. It is recommended that the beginner purchase as good a set of instruments as his means will permit, and that if his means are limited he purchase less than a full set of instruments, having the same of good quality.

All the instruments that need be used in the examples of this book are as follows:

A small spring bow-pen for circles, a lining pen or pen for straight lines, a small spring bow-pencil for circles, a large bow-pen with a removable leg to replace by a divider leg or a pencil leg, and having an extension piece to increase its capacity.

The spring bow-pen should have a stiff spring, and should be opened out to its full capacity to see that the spring acts well when so opened out, keeping the legs stiff when opened for the larger diameters. The purchaser should see that the joint for opening and closing the legs is an easy but not a loose fit on the screw, and that the legs will not move sideways. To test this latter, which is of great importance in the spring bow-pencil as well as in the pen, it is well to close the legs nearly together and taking one leg in one hand and the other leg in the other hand (between the forefinger and thumb), pushing and pulling them sideways, any motion in that direction being sufficient to condemn the instrument. It is safest and best to have the two legs of the bow-pen and pencil made from one piece of metal, and not of two separate pieces screwed together at the top, as the screw will rarely hold them firmly together. The points should be long and fine, and as round as possible. In very small instruments separate points that are fastened with a screw are objectionable, because, in very small circles, they hide the point and make it difficult to apply the instrument to the exact proper point or spot on the drawing.

The joints of the large bow or circle-pen should also be somewhat stiff, and quite free from side motion, and the extension piece should be rigidly secured when held by the screw. It is a good plan in purchasing to put in the extension piece, open the joint and the pen to their fullest, and draw a circle, moving the pen in one direction, and then redraw it, moving it in the other direction, and if one line only appears and that not thickened by the second drawing, the pen is a good one.

The lead pencil should be of hard lead, and it is recommended that they be of the H, H, H, H, H, H, in the English grades, which corresponds to the V, V, H, of the Dixon grade. The pencil lines should be made as lightly as possible; first, because the presence of the lead on the paper tends to prevent the ink from passing to the paper; and, secondly, because in rubbing out the pencil lines the ink lines are reduced in blackness and the surface of the paper becomes roughened, so that it will soil easier and be harder to clean. In order to produce fine pencil lines without requiring a very frequent sharpening of the pencil it is best to sharpen the pencil as in Figures 7 and 8, so that the edge shall be long in the direction in which it is moved, which is denoted by the arrow in Figure 7. But when very fine work is to be done, as in the case of Patent Office drawings, a long, round point is preferable, because the eye can see plainer just where the pencil will begin to mark and leave off; hence the pencil lines will not be so liable to overrun.

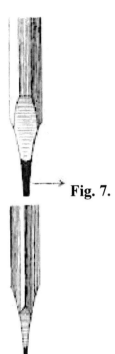

Fig. 7.

Fig. 8.

In place of the ordinary wood-covered lead pencils there may be obtained at the drawing material stores pencil holders for holding the fine, round sticks of lead, and these are by far the best for a learner. They are easier to sharpen, and will slip in the holder, giving warning when the draftsman is pressing them too hard on the paper, as he is apt to do. The best method of trimming these leads, as also lead pencils after they have been roughly shaped, is with a small fine file, holding the file still and moving the pencil; or a good piece of emery paper or sand paper is good, moving the pencil as before.

All lines in pencilling as in inking in should begin at the left hand and be drawn towards the right, or when triangles are used the lines are begun at the bottom and drawn towards the top or away from the operator. The rubber used should not be of a harsh grade, since that will roughen the face of the paper and probably cause the ink to run. The less rubbing out the better the learner will progress, and the more satisfaction he will receive from the results. If it becomes necessary to scratch out it is best done with a penknife well sharpened, and not applied too forcibly to the paper but somewhat lightly, and moved in different and not all in one direction. After the penknife the rubber may sometimes be used to advantage, since it will, if of a smooth grade, leave the paper smoother than the knife. Finally, before inking in, the surface that has been scraped should be condensed again by rubbing some clean, hard substance over it which will prevent the ink from spreading. The end of a paper-cutter or the end of a rounded ivory handled drawing instrument is excellent for this purpose.

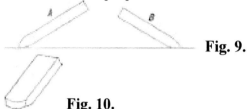

Fig. 9.

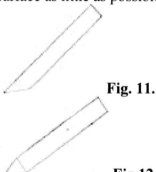

Fig. 10.

It is well to use the rubber for general purposes in such a way as to fit it for special purposes; thus, in cleaning the sheet of paper, the rubber may be applied first, as in Figure 9, as at A, and then as at B, and if it be moved sideways at the same time it will wear to the form shown in Figure 10, which will enable it to be applied along a line that may require to be rubbed out without removing other and neighboring lines. If the rubber is in the form of a square stick one end may be bevelled, as in Figure 11, which is an excellent form, or it may be made to have a point, as in Figure 12. The object is in each case to enable the rubber action to be confined to the desired location on the paper, so as to destroy its smooth surface as little as possible.

Fig. 11.

Fig 12.

For simple cleaning purposes, or to efface the pencil lines when they are drawn very lightly, squares of sponge-rubber answer admirably, these being furnished by the dealers in drawing materials.

A piece of bread will answer a similar purpose, but it is less convenient.

For glazed surface paper, as Bristol-board, the smoothest rubber must be used, the grade termed velvet rubber answering well.

THE DRAWING PAPER.

Whatever kind of drawing paper be used it should be kept dry, or the ink, however good it may be, will be apt to run and make a thick line that will not have the sharp, clean edges necessary to make lines look well.

Drawing paper is made in various qualities, kinds, and forms, as follows: The sizes and names of paper made in sheets are:

Cap, 13 × 16 inches.
Demy, 20 × 15 "
Medium, 22 × 17 "
Royal, 24 × 19 "
Super Royal, 27 × 19 "
Imperial, 30 × 21 "
Elephant, 28 × 22 "
Columbier, 34 × 23 "
Atlas, 33 × 26 "
Theorem, 34 × 28 "
Double Elephant, 40 × 26 "
Antiquarian, 52 × 31 "
Emperor, 40 × 60 "
Uncle Sam, 48 × 120 "

the thickness of the sheets increasing with their size. Some sheets of paper are hot pressed, to give a smoother surface, and thus enable cleaner-edged lines to be drawn.

Fig. 13.

For large drawings paper is made in rolls of various widths, but as rolled paper is troublesome to lay flat upon the drawing board, it is recommended to the learner to obtain the sheets, which may be laid sufficiently flat by means of broad headed pins, such as shown in Figure 13, which are called thumb tacks. These are forced through the paper into the board at each corner, as in Figure 14 at *f*. On account of the large diameter of the stems of these thumb tacks, which unduly pierce and damage the board, and on account also of their heads, by reason of their thickness, coming in the way of the square blade, it will be found preferable to use the smallest sizes of ordinary iron tacks, with flat heads, whose stems are much finer and heads much thinner than thumb tacks. The objection to ordinary tacks is that they are more difficult to remove, but they are, as stated, more desirable for use.

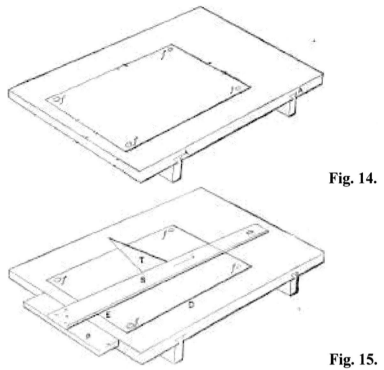

Fig. 14.

Fig. 15.

If the paper is nearly the full size of the board, it does not much matter as to its precise location on the board, but otherwise it is best to place it as near the left-hand edge of the board as convenient, as is shown in Figure 14.

The lower edge, D, Figure 15, of the paper, however, should not be placed too near the edge, A, of the board, because if the end P of the square back comes down below the edge of the board, it is more difficult to keep the square back true against the end of the board.

The paper must lie flat upon and close to the surface of the board, and a sufficient number of tacks must be used to effect this purpose.

Drawings that are to be intricate, or to contain a great many lines, as a drawing of an engine or of a machine, are best pasted or glued all around the edges of the paper, which should first be dampened; but as the learner will scarcely require to make such drawings until he is somewhat familiar with and well practised in the use of the instruments, this part of the subject need not be treated here.

TRACING PAPER.

For taking tracings from drawings tracing paper or tracing cloth is used. They require to be stretched tightly and without wrinkles upon the drawing. To effect this object the mucilage should be thick, and the tracing paper should be dampened with a sponge after it is pasted. It must be thoroughly dry before use, or the ink will run.

Tracing cloth must be fastened by pins or thumb tacks, and not dampened. The drawing should be made on the polished side of the cloth, and any coloring to be done should be on the other side, and done after the tracing is removed from the drawing.

THE INK.

India ink should always be used for mechanical drawing: First, because it lies upon and does not sink into the paper, and is, therefore, easily erased; and, secondly, because it does not corrode or injure the drawing instruments.

India ink is prepared in two forms—in the stick and in a liquid form. The stick ink is mixed in what are termed saucers, or cabinet saucers, one being placed above the other, so as to exclude the dust from settling in it, and also to prevent the rapid evaporation to which it is subject.

The surface of the saucer should be smooth, as any roughness grinds the ink too coarsely, whereas the finer it is ground or mixed the easier it will flow, the less liability to clog the instruments, and the smoother and more flat it will lie upon the paper. In mixing the ink only a small quantity of water should be used, the stick of ink being pressed *lightly* upon the saucer and moved quickly, the grinding being continued until the ink is mixed quite thickly. This will grind the ink fine as it is mixed, and more water may be added to thin it. It is best, however, to let the ink be somewhat thick for use, and to keep it covered when not in use; and though water may be added if it gets too thick, yet ink that has once dried should not be mixed up again, as it will not work so well after having once dried.

Of liquid inks the Higgins ink is by far the best, being quite equal to and much more convenient for use than the best stick ink.

The difference between a good and an inferior India ink lies chiefly in the extent to which the lamp-black, which is the coloring matter, forms with the water a chemical solution rather than a mechanical mixture. In inferior ink the lamp-black is more or less held in suspension, and by prolonged exposure to the air will separate, so that on being spread the solid particles will aggregate by themselves and the water by itself.

This explains why draughtsmen will, after the ink has been exposed to the air for an hour or two, add a drop of mucilage to it; the mucilage thickening the solution, adding weight to the water, and deferring the separation of the lamp-black.

A good India ink is jet black, flows easily, lies close to, does not stand upon or sink into the paper, and has an even lustre, the latter being an indication of fineness. The more perfect the incorporation of the lamp-black with the water the easier the ink will flow, the less liable it is to clog the instruments, the more even and sharp the edges of the lines, and the finer the lines that may be drawn.

Usually India ink can only be tested by actual trial; but since it is desirable to test before purchasing it, it may be mentioned that one method is to mix a little on the finger nail, and if it has a "bronzy" gloss it is a good indication. It should also spread out and dry without any tendency to separate.

The best method of testing is to mix a very little, and drop a single drop in a tumbler of clear water. The best ink will diffuse itself over the surface, and if the water is disturbed will diffuse itself through the water, leaving it translucent and black, with a slight tinge of bronze color. A coarser ink will act in a similar manner, but make the water somewhat opaque, with a blue-black, or dull, ashy color. A still coarser ink will, when diffused over the surface of the water, show fine specks, like black dust, on the surface. This is readily apparent, showing that the mixture of the ink is not homogeneous.

When it is an object to have the lines of a drawing show as black as possible, as for drawings that are to be photo-engraved, the ink should be mixed so thickly as to have a tendency to lift when a body, such as a lead pencil, is lifted out of it. For Patent Office drawings some will mix it so thickly that under the above test it appears a little stringy.

The thicker the ink can be used the better, because the tendency of the carbon to separate is less; and it is for this reason that the test mentioned with a tumbler of water is so accurate. When ink is to be used on parchment, or glossy tracing-paper, it will flow perfectly if a few drops of ox-gall be mixed with it; but on soft paper, or on bristol board, this will cause the ink to spread.

For purposes of measurement, there are special rules or scales of steel and of paper manufactured. The steel rules are finely and accurately divided, and some are of triangular form, so that when laid upon the paper the lines divided will lie close to the paper, and the light will fall directly on the ruled surface. Triangular rules or scales are therefore much superior to flat ones. The object of having a paper rule or scale is, that the paper will expand and contract under varying degrees of atmospheric moisture, the same as the drawing paper does.

Figure 16 represents a triangular scale, having upon it six different divisions of the inch. These are made in different patterns, having either decimal divisions or the vulgar fractions. Being made of steel, and nickel-plated, they are proof against the moisture of the fingers, and are not subject to the variation of the wooden scale.

Fig. 16.

CHAPTER II.

THE PREPARATION AND USE OF THE INSTRUMENTS.

The points of drawing instruments require to be very accurately prepared and shaped, to enable them to make clean, clear lines. The object is to have the points as sharp as they can be made without cutting the paper, and the curves as even and regular as possible.

Fig. 17.

Fig. 18.

The lining pen should be formed as in Figure 17, which presents an edge and a front view of the points. The inside faces should be flat across, and slightly curved in their lengths, as shown. If this curve is too great, as shown exaggerated in Figure 18, the body of the ink lies too near the point and is apt to flow too freely, running over the pen-point and making a thick, ragged line. On the other hand, if the inside faces, between which the ink lies, are too parallel and narrow near the points, the ink dries in the pen, and renders a too frequent cleaning necessary. Looking at the face of the pen as at A in Figure 17, its point should have an even curve, as shown, the edge being as sharp as it can be made without cutting the drawing paper. Upon this quality depends the fineness and cleanness of the lines it will make. This thin edge should extend around the curve as far as the dotted line, so that it will be practicable to slant the pen in either of the directions shown in Figure 19; and it is obvious that its thickness must be equal around the arc, so that the same thickness of line will be drawn whether the pen be held vertical or slanted in either direction.

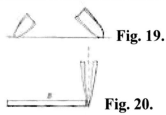 **Fig. 19.**

Fig. 20.

The outside faces of the pen should be slightly curved, so that when held vertically, as in Figure 20 (the dotted line representing the centre of the length of the instrument), and against the square blade S, the point will meet the paper a short distance from the lower edge of S as shown. By this means it is not necessary to adjust the square edge exactly coincident with the line, but a little way from it. This is an advantage for two reasons: first, the trouble of setting the square-edge exactly coincident is avoided, and, secondly, the liability of the ink to adhere to the edge of the square-blade and flow on to the paper and make a thick, ragged line, is prevented.

The square being set as near to the line as desired, the handle may be held at such an angle that the pen-point will just meet the line when sloped either as in Figure 21 or 22. If, however, the slope be too much in the direction shown in Figure 21, practice is necessary to enable the drawing of straight lines if they be long ones, because any variation in the angle of the instrument to the paper obviously vitiates the straightness of the line. If, on the other hand, the square be too close to the line, and the pen therefore requires to be sloped as in Figure 22, the ink flowing from the pen-point is apt to adhere to the square-edge, and the result will be a ragged, thick line, as shown in Figure 23.

 Fig. 21.

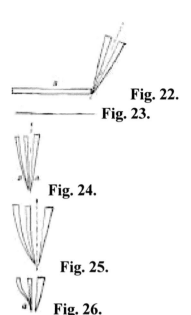

Fig. 22.

Fig. 23.

Fig. 24.

Fig. 25.

Fig. 26.

Each of the legs should be of equal thickness at the pen-point edge, so that when closed together the point will be in the middle of the edge. The width and curve of each individual point should be quite equal, and the easiest method of attaining this end is as follows:

Take a small slip of Arkansas oil-stone, and with the pen-points closed firmly by the screw trim the pen-edges to the required curve as shown at A, Figure 17, making the curve as even as possible. Then stone the faces until this curve is brought up to a sharp edge at the point between the two pen-legs forming the point.

Next take a piece of 000 French emery paper, lay it upon some flat body like the blade of a square, and smooth the curve of the edge enough to take off the fine, sharp edge left by the oil-stone; then apply the outside flat faces of the pen to the emery paper again, bringing the pen-edge up sharp.

The emery paper will simply have smoothed and polished the surfaces, still leaving them too sharp, so sharp as to cut the paper, and to take off this sharp edge (which must first be done on the inside faces) open the pen-points as wide as the screw will permit. Then wrap one thickness of the emery paper upon a thin blade, as upon a drawing-triangle, and pass the open pen-points over it, and move the instrument endwise, taking care to keep the inside face level with the surface of the emery paper, so that the pen-points shall not cut through. Next close the pen-points with the screw until they nearly, but not quite, touch, and sweep the edge of the pen-point along the emery paper under a slight pressure, so moving the handle that at each stroke the whole length around the curved end of the pen will meet the emery surface. During this motion the inside faces of the pen-point must be held as nearly vertical as possible, so as to keep the two halves of the pen-point equal.

The pen is now ready for use, and will draw a fine and clean line.

It is not usual to employ emery paper for the purpose indicated, but it will be found very desirable, since it leaves a smoother surface and edge than the oil-stone alone.

Circle-pens are more difficult to put in order than the straight-line pen, especially those for drawing the smallest circles, which cannot be well drawn unless the pen is of the precise right shape and in the best condition.

A circle-pen is shown in Figure 24, in which A represents the point-leg and B the pen-leg. The point-leg must be the longest because it requires to enter the drawing paper before the pen meets the surface. The point should be sharp and round, for any edges or angles on it will cause it to widen the hole in the paper when it is rotated. To shape the points to prevent the enlargement of the centre in the paper is one of the most important considerations in the use of this instrument, especially when several circles require to be drawn from the same centre. To accomplish this end the inside of the point-leg should be, as near as possible, parallel to the length of the instrument (which is denoted in Figure 24 by the dotted line) when the legs are closed, as in the figure. If the point is at an angle, as shown in Figure 25, it is obvious that rotating it will enlarge the top of the centre in the drawing paper. The point should be sharp and smooth on its circumferential surface, and so much longer than the pen-point that it will have sufficient hold in the paper when the instrument stands vertical and the pen-point meets the surface of it, which amount is about 1/64th of an inch.

We may now consider the shape of the pen-point. Its inside surfaces should be flat across and to the curve shown in Figure 24, not as shown exaggerated in Figure 25, because in the latter the body of the ink will be too near the pen-point, and but little can be placed in it without causing it sometimes to flow over the edges and down the outside of the pen.

A form of pen-point recently introduced is shaped as in Figure 26, the object being to have a thin stream of ink near the marking pen-point and the main body of the ink near at hand, instead of extending up the pen, as would be the case with Figure 24. The advantage thus gained is that the ink lies in a more solid body, and having less area of surface exposed to the air will not dry so quickly in the pen; but this is more than offset by the liability of the ink to flow over the crook at A, and cause the pen to draw a thick ragged line. The pen-point must be slightly inclined toward the needle-point, to the end that they may approach each other close enough for drawing very small circles, but it should also stand as nearly vertical as will permit that end to be attained. As this pen is for drawing small circles only, it does not require much ink, and hence may be somewhat close together, as in Figure 24; this has the advantage that the point is not hidden from observation.

In forming the pen-point the greatest refinement is necessary to enable the drawing of very small true circles, say 1/16th of an inch, or less, in diameter. The requirements are that the pen-point shall meet the surface of the paper when the needle-point has entered it sufficiently to give the necessary support, and that the instrument shall stand vertical, as shown by the dotted line in Figure 24. Also, that the pen shall then touch the paper at a point only, this point being the apex of a fine curve; that this curve be equal on each side of the point of contact with the paper; that both halves forming the pen be of equal thickness and width at the pointed curve; and that the point be as sharp as possible without cutting the paper.

The best method of attaining these ends is as follows: On each side of the pen make, with an oil-stone, a flat place, as C D, Figure 27 (where the pen-point is shown magnified), thus bringing both halves to an edge of exactly equal length, and leaving the point flat at D. These flat places must be parallel to one another and to the joint between the two halves of the pen. As the oil-stone may leave a slightly ragged edge, it is a good plan to take a piece of 00 French emery paper, lay it on a flat surface, and holding the instrument vertically remove the fine edge D until it will not cut. Then with the oil-stone shape the curved edge as in Figure 28, taking care that the curve no more than brings the flat place D up to a true curve and leaves the edge sharp, with only the very point touching the paper, which is represented in the cut by the horizontal line.

Figure 27.

Figure 28.

Figure 29.

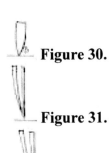 **Figure 30.**

Figure 31.

Figure 32.

The point must have a sharp edge all around the curve, and the two halves must be exactly equal in width, for if one half is wider than the other, as in Figure 29 at a, or as in Figure 30 at b, it will be impossible to draw a very small circle true. So, likewise, the two halves of the pen must be of exactly equal length, and not one half longer than the other, as in Figures 31 or 32, which would tend to cut the paper, and also render the drawing of true small circles impracticable.

When the pen is closed to draw a very small circle the two halves of the pen-leg should have an equal degree of contact with the surface of the paper, and then as the legs are opened out to draw larger circles the contact of the outside half of the pen will have less contact with the paper. The smaller the circle, the more difficult it is to keep the point-leg from slipping out of the centre, and the more difficult it is to draw a clear line and true circle; hence the points should be shaped to the best advantage for drawing these small circles, by oil-stoning the pen, as already described, and then finishing it as follows:

After the oil-stoning, open the two valves of the pen-leg wide enough to admit a piece of 000 French emery paper wrapped once around a very thin blade, and move the pen endwise as described for the straight-line pen. This will smooth the inner surfaces and remove any fine wire-edge that the oil-stone may leave. Close the two halves of the pen again, and lightly emery-paper the outside faces, which will leave the edge sharp enough to cut the paper. The removal of the sharp edge still left, to the exact degree, requires great care. It may best be done by closing the pen until its two halves very nearly, but not quite, touch, then adjust it to mark a circle of about 3/16 inch diameter, and strike a number of circles in different locations upon the surface of a piece of 0000 French emery paper.

In marking these circles, however, let the instrument stand out of the perpendicular, and do very little while standing vertically.

Indeed, it is well to strike a number of half-circles, first from right to left and then from left to right, and finally draw a full circle, sloping the pen on one side, gradually raising it vertically, and finally sloping it to the other side. This will insure that the pen has contact at its extreme point, and leave that point fine and keen, but not enough so to cut the paper. To test the pen, draw small circles with the pen rotated first in one direction and then in the other, closing its points so as to mark a fine line, which, if the pen is properly shaped, will be clear and fine, while if improperly formed the circle drawn with the pen rotated in one direction will not coincide with that drawn while rotating it in the other. The same circle may be drawn over several times to make a thorough test. If a drawing instrument will draw a fine line correctly, it will be found to answer for thick lines which are more easily made.

In thus preparing the instruments, the operator will find that if he occasionally holds the points in the right position with regard to the light, he will be able to see plainly if the work is proceeding evenly and equally, for if one-half of the pen is thicker at the point or edge than the other, it will show a brighter line. This is especially the case with instruments that have become dull by use, for in that case the edges will be found quite bright, and any inequality of thickness shows plainly.

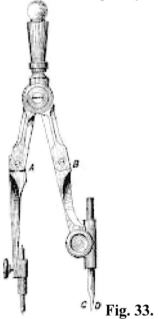

Fig. 33.

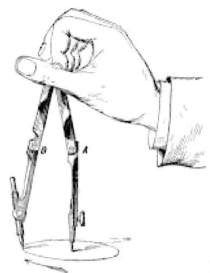

Fig. 34.

It follows, from what has been said, that the needle-point and pen-point should stand vertical when in use, and to effect this the instruments, except in the smallest sizes, are provided with joints, such as shown at A and B in the bow-pencil or circle-pencil, in Figure 33. These joints should be sufficiently stiff that they will not move too easily, and yet will move rather than that the legs should sensibly spring without moving at the joint. The needle-point leg should be adjusted by means of the joint, to stand vertical, and the same remarks apply equally to the pen-leg; but in the case of the pencil-leg it is the pencil itself and not the leg that requires attention, the joint B being so adjusted that the pencil either stands vertical, or, what is perhaps preferable, so that it stands inclined slightly towards the needle-point. In sharpening the pencil the inner face C may be made concave or at least vertical and flat, and the outer convex or else bevelled and flat, producing a fine and long edge rounded in its length of edge. In using the circle-pencil and circle-pen it will be found more convenient to rotate it in the direction of the arrow in Figure 34. It should be held lightly to the paper, and the learner will find that he has a natural tendency to hold it too firmly and press it too heavily, which is *especially to be avoided*.

If in drawing a small circle the needle-point slips out of the paper, it is because the pencil-point is too long; or, what is the same thing, the needle-point does not protrude far enough out from the leg. Or if the instrument requires to be leaned over too much to make the pencil or pen mark, it is because the pen or pencil is not far enough out, and this again may cause the needle-point to slip out of the paper.

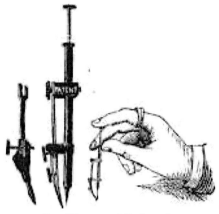

Fig. 35.

In Figure 35 is shown a German instrument especially designed to avoid this slipping. The peculiarity of this instrument consists in the arrangement of the centre point, which remains stationary whilst the pen or pencil, resting by its own weight on the paper, is guided round by gently turning, without pressure, the small knob at the upper end of the tube. By this means the misplacing or sliding of the centre-point and the cutting of the paper by the pen are avoided. By means of this fixed centre-point any number of concentric circles may be drawn, without making a hole of very distinguishable size on the paper.

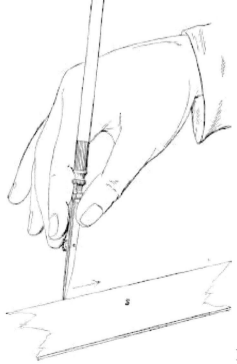

Fig 36.

Fig 37.

In applying the ink to the bow-pen as to all other instruments, care must be taken that the ink lies between the points only and not on the outside, for in the latter case the ink will flow down too freely and make a broad, ragged line, perhaps getting on the edge of the square blade or triangle, and causing a blot of ink on the drawing.

In using a straight line or lining pen with a T square it may be used as in Figure 36, being nearly vertical, as shown, and moved from left to right as denoted by the arrow, S representing the square blade. But in using it, or a pencil, with a straight edge or a triangle unsupported by the square blade, the latter should be steadied by letting the fingers rest upon it while using the instrument, the operation being shown in Figure 37. The position, Figure 36, is suitable for long lines, and that in Figure 37 for small drawings, where the pen requires close adjustment to the lines.

CHAPTER III.

LINES AND CURVES.

Although the beginner will find that a study of geometry is not essential to the production of such elementary examples of mechanical drawing as are given in this book, yet as more difficult examples are essayed he will find such a study to be of great advantage and assistance. Meantime the following explanation of simple geometrical terms is all that is necessary to an understanding of the examples given.

The shortest distance between two points is termed the radius; and, in the case of a circle, means the distance from the centre to the perimeter measured in a straight line.

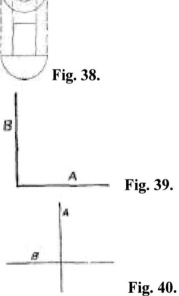

Fig. 38.

Fig. 39.

Fig. 40.

Dotted lines, thus, <——- >, mean the direction and the points at which a dimension is taken or marked. Dotted lines, thus,——-, simply connect the same parts or lines in different views of the object. Thus in Figure 38 are a side and an end view of a rivet, and the dotted lines show that the circles on the end view correspond to the circle of the diameters of the head and of the stem, and therefore represent their diameters while showing that both are round. A straight line is in geometry termed a right line.

A line at a right angle to another is said to be perpendicular to it; thus, in Figures 39, 40, and 41, lines A are in each case perpendicular to line B, or line B is in each case perpendicular to line A.

A point is a position or location supposed to have no size, and in cases where necessary is indicated by a dot.

Parallel lines are those equidistant one from the other throughout their length, as in Figure 42. Lines maybe parallel though not straight; thus, in Figure 43, the lines are parallel.

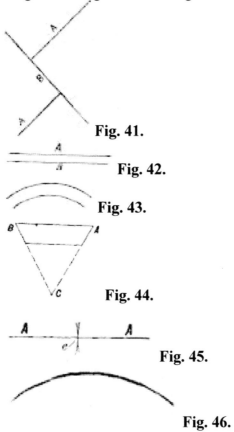

Fig. 41.

Fig. 42.

Fig. 43.

Fig. 44.

Fig. 45.

Fig. 46.

A line is said to be *produced* when it is extended beyond its natural limits: thus, in Figure 44, lines A and B are *produced* in the point C.

A line is bisected when the centre of its length is marked: thus, line A in Figure 45 is bisected, at or in, as it is termed, *e*.

The line bounding a circle is termed its circumference or periphery and sometimes the perimeter.

A part of this circumference is termed an arc of a circle or an arc; thus Figure 46 represents an arc. When this arc has breadth it is termed a segment; thus Figures 47 and 48 are segments of a circle. A straight line cutting off an arc is termed the chord of the arc; thus, in Figure 48, line A is the chord of the arc.

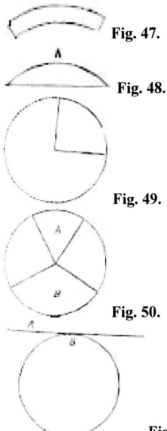

Fig. 47.

Fig. 48.

Fig. 49.

Fig. 50.

Fig. 51.

A quadrant of a circle is one quarter of the same, being bounded on two of its sides by two radial lines, as in Figure 49.

When the area of a circle that is enclosed within two radial lines is either less or more than one quarter of the whole area of the circle the figure is termed a sector; thus, in Figure 50, A and B are both sectors of a circle.

A straight line touching the perimeter of a circle is said to be tangent to that circle, and the point at which it touches is that to which it is tangent; thus, in Figure 51, line A is tangent to the circle at point B. The half of a circle is termed a semicircle; thus, in Figure 52, A B and C are each a semicircle.

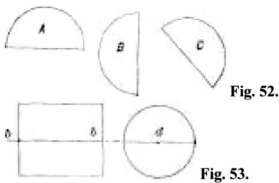

Fig. 52.

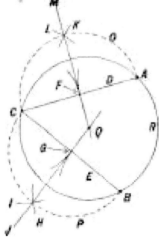

Fig. 53.

The point from which a circle or arc of a circle is drawn is termed its centre. The line representing the centre of a cylinder is termed its axis; thus, in Figure 53, dot *d* represents the centre of the circle, and line *b b* the axial line of the cylinder.

To draw a circle that shall pass through any three given points: Let A B and C in Figure 54 be the points through which the circumference of a circle is to pass. Draw line D connecting A to C, and line E connecting B to C. Bisect D in F and E in G. From F as a centre draw the semicircle O, and from G as a centre draw the semicircle P; these two semicircles meeting the two ends of the respective lines D E. From B as a centre draw arc H, and from C the arc I, bisecting P in J. From A as a centre draw arc K, and from C the arc L, bisecting the semicircle O in M. Draw a line passing through M and F, and a line passing through J and Q, and where these two lines intersect, as at Q, is the centre of a circle R that will pass through all three of the points A B and C.

Fig. 54.

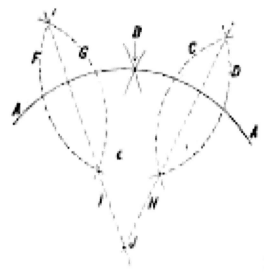

Fig. 55.

To find the centre from which an arc of a circle has been struck: Let A A in Figure 55 be the arc whose centre is to be found. From the extreme ends of the arc bisect it in B. From end A draw the arc C, and from B the arc D. Then from the end A draw arc G, and from B the arc F. Draw line H passing through the two points of intersections of arcs C D, and line I passing through the two points of intersection of F G, and where H and I meet, as at J, is the centre from which the arc was drawn.

A degree of a circle is the 1/360 part of its circumference. The whole circumference is supposed to be divided into 360 equal divisions, which are called the degrees of a circle; but, as one-half of the circle is simply a repetition of the other half, it is not necessary for mechanical purposes to deal with more than one-half, as is done in Figure 56. As the whole circle contains 360 degrees, half of it will contain one-half of that number, or 180; a quarter will contain 90, and an eighth will contain 45 degrees. In the protractors (as the instruments having the degrees of a circle marked on them are termed) made for sale the edges of the half-circle are marked off into degrees and half-degrees; but it is sufficient for the purpose of this explanation to divide off one quarter by lines 10 degrees apart, and the other by lines 5 degrees apart. The diameter of the circle obviously makes no difference in the number of decrees contained in any portion of it. Thus, in the quarter from 0 to 90, there are 90 degrees, as marked; but suppose the diameter of the circle were that of inner circle *d*, and one-quarter of it would still contain 90 degrees.

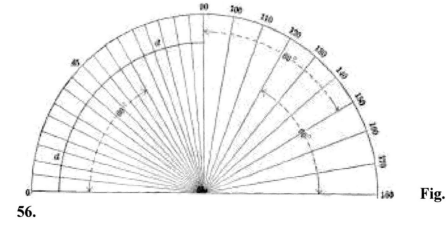

Fig. 56.

So, likewise, the degrees of one line to another are not always taken from one point, as from the point O, but from any one line to another. Thus the line marked 120 is 60 degrees from line 180, or line 90 is 60 degrees from line 150. Similarly in the other quarter of the circle 60 degrees are marked. This may be explained further by stating that the point O or zero may be situated at the point from which the degrees of angle are to be taken. Here it may be remarked that, to save writing the word "degrees," it is usual to place on the right and above the figures a small °, as is done in Figure 56, the 60° meaning sixty degrees, the °, of course, standing for degrees.

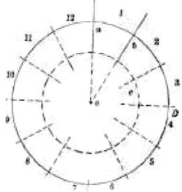

Fig. 57.

Suppose, then, we are given two lines, as *a* and *b* in Figure 57, and are required to find their angle one to the other. Then, if we have a protractor, we may apply it to the lines and see how many degrees of angle they contain. This word "contain" means how many degrees of angle there are between the lines, which, in the absence of a protractor, we may find by prolonging the lines until they meet in a point as at *c*. From this point as a centre we draw a circle D, passing through both lines *a*, *b*. All we now have to do is to find what part, or how much of the circumference, of the circle is enclosed within the two lines. In the example we find it is the one-twelfth part; hence the lines are 30 degrees apart, for, as the whole circle contains 360, then one-twelfth must contain 30, because $360 \div 12 = 30$.

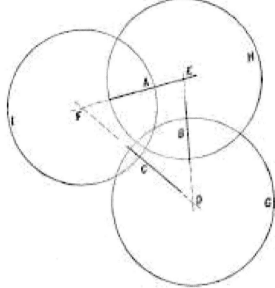

Fig. 58.

If we have three lines, as lines A B and C in Figure 58, we may find their angles one to the other by projecting or prolonging the lines until they meet as at points D, E, and F, and use these points as the centres wherefrom to mark circles as G, H, and I. Then, from circle H, we may, by dividing it, obtain the angle of A to B or of B to A. By dividing circle I we may obtain the angle of A to C or of C to A, and by dividing circle G we may obtain the angle of B to C or of C to B.

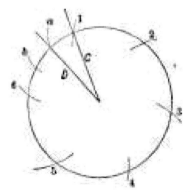

Fig. 59.

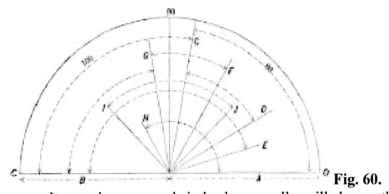

Fig. 60.

It may happen, and, indeed, generally will do so, that the first attempt will not succeed, because the distance between the lines measured, or the arc of the circle, will not divide the circle without having the last division either too long or too short, in which case the circle may be divided as follows: The compasses set to its radius, or half its diameter, will divide the circle into 6 equal divisions, and each of these divisions will contain 60 degrees of angle, because 360 (the number of degrees in the whole circle) ÷6 (the number of divisions) = 60, the number of degrees in each division. We may, therefore, subdivide as many of the divisions as are necessary for the two lines whose degrees of angle are to be found. Thus, in Figure 59, are two lines, C, D, and it is required to find their angle one to the other. The circle is divided into six divisions, marked respectively from 1 to 6, the division being made from the intersection of line C with the circle. As both lines fall within less than a division, we subdivide that division as by arcs *a*, *b*, which divide it into three equal divisions, of which the lines occupy one division. Hence, it is clear that they are at an angle of 20 degrees, because twenty is one-third of sixty. When the number of degrees of angle between two lines is less than 90, the lines are said to form an acute angle one to the other, but when they are at more than 90 degrees of angle they are said to form an obtuse angle. Thus, in Figure 60, A and C are at an acute angle, while B and C are at an obtuse angle. F and G form an acute angle one to the other, as also do G and B, while H and A are at an obtuse angle. Between I and J there are 90 degrees of angle; hence they form neither an acute nor an obtuse angle, but what is termed a right-angle, or an angle of 90 degrees. E and B are at an obtuse angle. Thus it will be perceived that it is the amount of inclination of one line to another that determines its angle, irrespective of the positions of the lines, with respect to the circle.

TRIANGLES.

A right-angled triangle is one in which two of the sides are at a right angle one to the other. Figure 61 represents a right-angled triangle, A and B forming a right angle. The side opposite, as C, is called the hypothenuse. The other sides, A and B, are called respectively the base and the perpendicular.

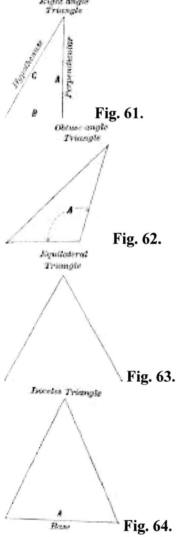

Fig. 61.

Fig. 62.

Fig. 63.

Fig. 64.

An acute-angled triangle has all its angles acute, as in Figure 63.

An obtuse-angled triangle has one obtuse angle, as A, Figure 62.

When all the sides of a triangle are equal in length and the angles are all equal, as in Figure 63, it is termed an equilateral triangle, and either of its sides may be called the base. When two only of the sides and two only of the angles are equal, as in Figure 64, it is termed an isosceles triangle, and the side that is unequal, as

A in the figure, is termed the base.

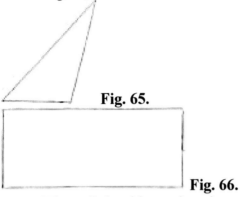

Fig. 65.

Fig. 66.

When all the sides and angles are unequal, as in Figure 65, it is termed a scalene triangle, and either of its sides may be called the base.

The angle opposite the base of a triangle is called the vertex.

Fig. 67.

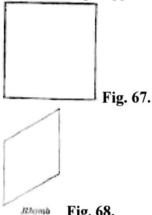

Rhomb **Fig. 68.**

A figure that is bounded by four straight lines is termed a quadrangle, quadrilateral or tetragon. When opposite sides of the figure are parallel to each other it is termed a parallelogram, no matter what the angle of the adjoining lines in the figure may be. When all the angles are right angles, as in Figure 66, the figure is called a rectangle. If the sides of a rectangle are of equal length, as in Figure 67, the figure is called a square. If two of the parallel sides of a rectangle are longer than the other two sides, as in Figure 66, it is called an oblong. If the length of the sides of a parallelogram are all equal and the angles are not right angles, as in Figure 68, it is called a rhomb, rhombus or diamond. If two of the parallel sides of a parallelogram are longer than the other two, and the angles are not right angles, as in Figure 69, it is called a rhomboid. If two of the parallel sides of a quadrilateral are of unequal lengths and the angles of the other two sides are not equal, as in Figure 70, it is termed a trapezoid.

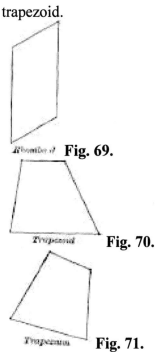

Fig. 69.

Rhomboid

Fig. 70.

Trapezoid

Fig. 71.

Trapezium

If none of the sides of a quadrangle are parallel, as in Figure 71, it is termed a trapezium.

THE CONSTRUCTION OF POLYGONS.

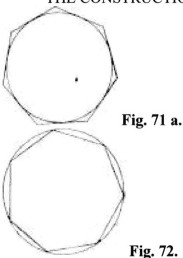

Fig. 71 a.

Fig. 72.

The term polygon is applied to figures having flat sides equidistant from a common centre. From this centre a circle may be struck that will touch all the corners of the sides of the polygon, or the point of each side that is central in the length of the side. In drawing a polygon, one of these circles is used upon which to divide the figure into the requisite number of divisions for the sides. When the dimension of the polygon across its corners is given, the circle drawn to that dimension circumscribes the polygon, because the circle is without or outside of the polygon and touches it at its corners only. When the dimension across the flats of the polygon is given, or when the dimension given is that of a circle that can be inscribed or marked within the polygon, touching its sides but not passing through them, then the polygon circumscribes or envelops the circle, and the circle is inscribed or marked within the polygon. Thus, in Figure 71 *a*, the circle is inscribed within the polygon, while in Figure 72 the polygon is circumscribed by the circle; the first is therefore a circumscribed and the second an inscribed polygon. A regular polygon is one the sides of which are all of an equal length.

NAMES OF REGULAR POLYGONS.

A figure of 3 sides is called a Trigon. " 4 " Tetragon. polygon 5 " Pentagon. " 6 " Hexagon. " 7 " Heptaagon. " 8 " Octagon. " 9 " Enneagon or Nonagon.

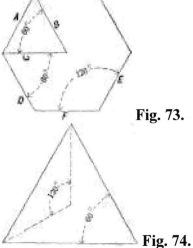

Fig. 73.

Fig. 74.

The angles of regular polygons are designated by their degrees of angle, "at the centre" and "at the circumference." By the angle at the centre is meant the angle of a side to a radial line; thus in Figure 73 is a hexagon, and at C is a radial line; thus the angle of the side D to C is 60 degrees. Or if at the two ends of a side, as A, two radial lines be drawn, as B, C, then the angles of these two lines, one to the other, will be the "angle at the centre." The angle at the circumference is the angle of one side to its next neighbor; thus the angle at the circumference in a hexagon is 120 degrees, as shown in the figure for the sides E, F. It is obvious that as all the sides are of equal length, they are all at the same angle both to the centre and to one another. In Figure 74 is a trigon, the angles at its centre being 120, and the angle at the circumference being 60, as marked.

The angles of regular polygons:

Trigon, at the centre, 120°, at the circumference, 60°. Tetragon, " 90°, " " 90°. Pentagon, " 72°, " " 108°. Hexagon, " 60°, " " 120°. Octagon, " 45°, " " 135°. Enneagon, " 40°, " " 140°. Decagon, " 36°, " " 144°. Dodecagon, " 30°, " " 150°.

THE ELLIPSE.

An ellipse is a figure bounded by a continuous curve, whose nature will be shown presently.

The dimensions of an ellipse are taken at its extreme length and narrowest width, and they are designated in three ways, as by the length and breadth, by the major and minor axis (the major axis meaning the length, and the minor the breadth of the figure), and the conjugate and transverse diameters, the transverse meaning the shortest, and the conjugate the longest diameter of the figure.

In this book the terms major and minor axis will be used to designate the dimensions.

The minor and major axes are at a right angle one to the other, and their point of intersection is termed the axis of the ellipse.

In an ellipse there are two points situated upon the line representing the major axis, and which are termed the foci when both are spoken of, and a focus when one only is referred to, foci simply being the plural of focus. These foci are equidistant from the centre of the ellipse, which is formed as follows: Two pins are driven in on the major axis to represent the foci A and B, Figure 75, and around these pins a loop of fine twine is passed; a pencil point, C, is then placed in the loop and pulled outwards, to take up the slack of the twine. The pencil is held vertical and moved around, tracing an ellipse as shown.

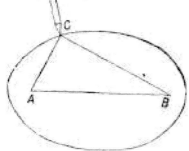

Fig. 75.

Now it is obvious, from this method of construction, that there will be at every point in the pencil's path a length of twine from the final point to each of the foci, and a length from one foci to the other, and the length of twine in the loop remaining constant, it is demonstrated that if in a true ellipse we take any number of points in its curve, and for each point add together its distance to each focus, and to this add the distance apart of the foci, the total sum obtained will be the same for each point taken.

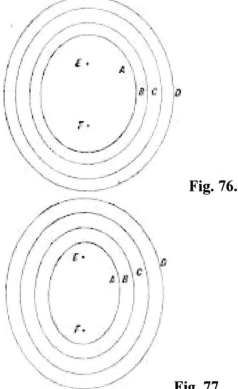

Fig. 76.

Fig. 77.

In Figures 76 and 77 are a series of ellipses marked with pins and a piece of twine, as already described. The corresponding ellipses, as A in both figures, were marked with the same loop, the difference in the two forms being due to the difference in distance apart of the foci. Again, the same loop was used for ellipses B in both figures, as also for C and D. From these figures we perceive that—

1st. With a given width or distance apart of foci, the larger the dimensions are the nearer the form of the figure will approach to that of a circle.

2d. The nearer the foci are together in an ellipse, having any given dimensions, the nearer the form of the figure will approach that of a circle.

3d. That the proportion of length to width in an ellipse is determined by the distance apart of the foci.

4th. That the area enclosed within an ellipse of a given

circumference is greater in proportion as the distance apart of the foci is diminished; and,

5th. That an ellipse may be given any required proportion of width to length by locating the foci at the requisite distance apart.

The form of a true ellipse may be very nearly approached by means of the arcs of circles, if the centres from which those arcs are struck are located in the most desirable positions for the form of ellipse to be drawn.

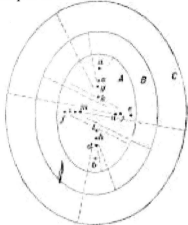

Fig. 78.

Thus in Figure 78 are three ellipses whose forms were pencilled in by means of pins and a loop of twine, as already described, but which were inked in by finding four arcs of circles of a radius that would most closely approach the pencilled line; *a b* are the foci of all three ellipses A, B, and C; the centre for the end curves of *a* are at *c* and *d*, and those for its side arcs are at *e* and *f*. For B the end centres are at *g* and *h*, and the side centres at *i* and *j*. For C the end centres are at *k*, *l*, and the side centres at *m* and *n*. It will be noted that, first, all the centres for the end curves fall on the line of the length or major axis, while all those for the sides fall on the line of width or the minor axis; and, second, that as the dimensions of the ellipses increase, the centres for the arcs fall nearer to the axis of the ellipse. Now in proportion as a greater number of arcs of circles are employed to form the figure, the nearer it will approach the form of a true ellipse; but in practice it is not usual to employ more than eight, while it is obvious that not less than four can be used. When four are used they will always fall somewhere on the lines on the major and minor axis; but if eight are used, two will fall on the line of the major axis, two on the line of the minor axis, and the remaining four elsewhere.

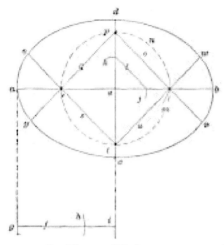

Fig. 79.

In Figure 79 is a construction wherein four arcs are used. Draw the line *a b*, the major axis, and at a right angle to it the line *c d*, the minor axis of the figure. Now find the difference between the length of half the two axes as shown below the figure, the length of line *f* (from *g* to *i*) representing half the length of the figure (as from *a* to *e*), and the length or radius from *g* to *h* equalling that from *e* to *d*; hence from *h* to *i* is the difference between half the major and half the minor axis. With the radius (*h i*), mark from *e* as a centre the arcs *j k*, and join *j k* by line *l*. Take half the length of line *l* and from *j* as a centre mark a line on *a* to the arc *m*. Now the radius of *m* from *e* will be the radius of all the centres from which to draw the figure; hence we may draw in the circle *m* and draw line *s*, cutting the circle. Then draw line *o*, passing through *m*, and giving the centre *p*. From *p* we draw the line *q*, cutting the intersection of the circle with line *a* and giving the centre *r*. From *r* we draw line *s*, meeting the circle and the line *c, d*, giving us the centre *t*. From *t* we draw line *u*, passing through the centre *m*. These four lines *o, q, s, u* are prolonged past the centres, because they define what part of the curve is to be drawn from each centre: thus from centre *m* the curve from *v* to *w* is drawn, from centre *t* the curve from *w* to *x* is drawn. From centre *r* the curve from *x* to *y* is drawn, and from centre *p* the curve from *y* to *v* is drawn. It is to be noted, however, that after the point *m* is found, the remaining lines may be drawn very quickly, because the line *o* from *m* to *p* may be drawn with the triangle of 45 degrees resting on the square blade. The triangle may be turned over, set to point *p* and line *q* drawn, and by turning the triangle again the line *s* may be drawn from point *r*; finally the triangle may be again turned over and line *u* drawn, which renders the drawing of the circle *m* unnecessary.

To draw an elliptical figure whose proportion of width to breadth shall remain the same, whatever the length of the major axis may be: Take any square figure and bisect it by the line A in Figure 80. Draw, in each half of the square, the diagonals E F, G H. From P as a centre with the radius P R draw the arc S E R. With the same radius draw from O as a centre the arc T D V. With radius L C draw arc R C V, and from K as a centre draw arc S B T.

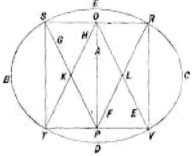

Fig. 80.

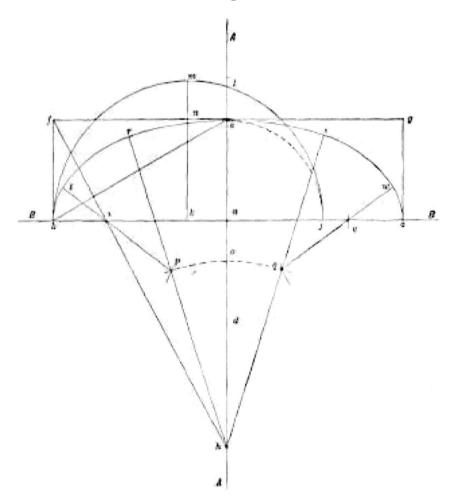

Fig. 81.

A very near approach to the true form of a true ellipse may be drawn by the construction given in Figure 81, in which A A and B B are centre lines passing through the major and minor axis of the ellipse, of which *a* is the axis or centre, *b c* is the major axis, and *a e* half the minor axis. Draw the rectangle *b f g c*, and then the diagonal line *b e*; at a right angle to *b e* draw line *f h*, cutting B B at *i*. With radius *a e* and from *a* as a centre draw the dotted arc *e j*, giving the point *j* on line B B. From centre *k*, which is on the line B B and central between *b* and *j*, draw the semicircle *b m j*, cutting A A at *l*. Draw the radius of the semicircle *b m j*, cutting it at *m*, and cutting *f g* at *n*. With the radius *m n* mark on A A at and from *a* as a centre the point *o*. With radius *h o* and from centre *h* draw the arc *p o q*. With radius *a l* and from *b* and *c* as centres, draw arcs cutting *p o q* at the points *p q*. Draw the lines *h p r* and *h q s* and also the lines *p i t* and *q v w*. From *h* as a centre draw that part of the ellipse lying between *r* and *s*, with radius *p r*; from *p* as a centre draw that part of the ellipse lying between *r* and *t*, with radius *q s*, and from *q* as a centre draw the ellipse from *s* to *w*, with radius *i t*; and from *i* as a centre draw the ellipse from *t* to *b* and with radius *v w*, and from *v* as a centre draw the ellipse from *w* to *c*, and one-half of the ellipse will be drawn. It will be seen that the whole construction has been performed to find the centres *h*, *p*, *q*, *i* and *v*, and that while *v* and *i* may be used to carry the curve around on the other side of the ellipse, new centres must be provided for *h p* and *q*, these new centres corresponding in position to *h p q*. Divesting the drawing of all the lines except those determining its dimensions and the centres from which the ellipse is struck, we have in Figure 82 the same ellipse drawn half as large. The centres *v*, *p*, *q*, *h* correspond to the same centres in Figure 81, while *v'*, *p'*, *q'*, *h'* are in corresponding positions to draw in the other half of the ellipse. The length of curve drawn from each centre is denoted by the dotted lines radiating from that centre; thus, from *h* the part from *r* to *s* is drawn; from *h'* that part from *r'* to *s'*. At the ends the respective centres *v* are used for the parts from *w* to *w'* and from *t* to *t'* respectively.

The most correct method of drawing an ellipse is by means of an instrument termed a trammel, which is shown in Figure 83. It consists of a cross frame in which are two grooves, represented by the broad black lines, one of which is at a right angle to the other. In these grooves are closely fitted two sliding blocks, carrying pivots E F, which may be fastened to the sliding blocks, while leaving them free to slide in the grooves at any adjusted distance apart. These blocks carry an arm or rod having a tracing point (as pen or pencil) at G.

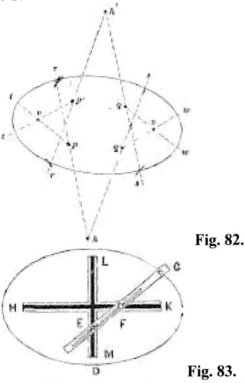

Fig. 82.

Fig. 83.

When this arm is swept around by the operator, the blocks slide in the grooves and the pen-point describes an ellipse whose proportion of width to length is determined by the distance apart of the sliding blocks, and whose dimensions are determined by the distance of the pen-point from the sliding block. To set the instrument, draw lines representing the major and minor axes of the required ellipse, and set off on these lines (equidistant from their intersection), to mark the required length and width of ellipse. Place the trammel so that the centre of its slots is directly over the point or centre from which the axes are marked (which may be done by setting the centres of the slots true to the lines passing through the axis) and set the pivots as follows: Place the pencil-point G so that it coincides with one of the points as C, and place the pivot E so that it comes directly at the point of intersection of the two slots, and fasten it there. Then turn the arm so that the pencil-point G coincides with one of the points of the minor axis as D, the arm lying parallel to B D, and place the pivot F over the centre of the trammel and fasten it there, and the setting is complete.

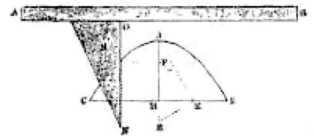

Fig. 84.

To draw a parabola mechanically: In Figure 84 C D is the width and H J the height of the curve. Bisect H D in K. Draw the diagonal line J K and draw K E, cutting K at a right angle to J K, and produce it in E. With the radius H E, and from J as a centre, mark point F, which will be the focus of the curve. At any convenient distance above J fasten a straight-edge A B, setting it parallel to the base C D of the parabola. Place a square S with its back against the straight-edge, setting the edge O N coincident with the line J H. Place a pin in the focus F, and tie to it one end of a piece of twine. Place a tracing-point at J, pass the twine around the tracing-point, bringing down along the square-blade and fasten it at N, with the tracing-point kept against the edge of the square and the twine kept taut; slide the square along the straight-edge, and the tracing-point will mark the half J C of the parabola. Turn the square over and repeat the operation to trace the other half J D. This method corresponds to the method of drawing an ellipse by the twine and pins, as already described.

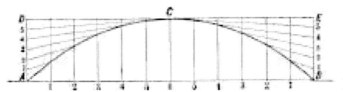

Fig. 85.

To draw a parabola by lines: Bisect the width A B in Figure 85, and divide each half into any convenient number of equal divisions; and through these points of division draw vertical lines, as 1, 2, 3, etc. (in each half). Divide the height A D at one end and B E at the other into as many equal divisions as the half of A B is divided into. From the points of divisions 1, 2, 3, etc., on lines A D and B E, draw lines pointing to C, and where these lines intersect the corresponding vertical lines are points through which the curve may be drawn. Thus on the side A D of the curve, the intersection of the two lines marked 1 is a point in the curve; the intersection of the two lines marked 2 is another point in the curve, and so on.

TO DRAW A HEART CAM.

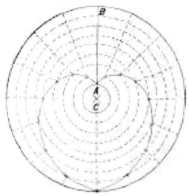

Fig. 86.

Draw the line A B, Figure 86, equal to the length of stroke required. Divide it into any number of equal parts, and from C as a centre draw circles through the points of division. Draw the outer circle and divide its circumference into twice as many equal divisions as the line A B was divided into. Draw radial lines from each point of division on the circle, and the points of intersection of the radial lines with the circles are points for the outline of the cam, and through these points a curved line may be drawn giving the shape of the cam. It is obvious that the greater the number of divisions on A B, the more points and the more perfect the curve may be drawn.

CHAPTER IV.

SHADOW LINES AND LINE SHADING.

SECTION LINING OR CROSS-HATCHING.

When the interior of a piece is to be shown as a piece cut in half, or when a piece is broken away, as is done to make more of the parts show, or show more clearly, the surface so broken away or cut off is section-lined or cross-hatched; that is to say, diagonal lines are drawn across it, and to distinguish one piece from another these lines are drawn at varying angles and of varying widths apart. In Figure 87 is given a view of three cylindrical pieces. It may be known to be a sectional view by the cross-hatching or section lines. It would be a difficult matter to represent the three pieces put together without showing them in section, because, in an outline view, the collars and recesses would not appear. Each piece could of course be drawn separately, but this would not show how they were placed when put together. They could be shown in one view if they were shaded by lines and a piece shown broken out where the collars and, recesses are, but line shading is too tedious for detail drawings, beside involving too much labor in their production.

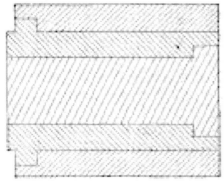 **Fig. 87.**

Figure 88 represents a case in which there are three cylindrical pieces one within the other, the two inner ones being fastened together by a screw which is shown dotted in in the end view, and whose position along the pieces is shown in the side view. The edges of the fracture in the outer piece are in this case cross-hatched, to show the line of fracture.

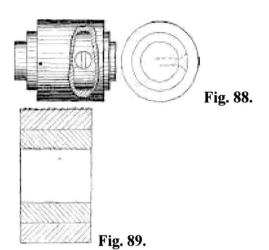

Fig. 88.

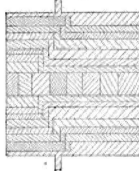

Fig. 89.

In cross-hatching it is better that the diagonal lines do not quite meet the edges of the piece, than that they should in the least overrun, as is shown in Figure 89, where in the top half the diagonals slightly overrun, while in the lower half they do not quite meet the outlines of the piece.

In Figure 90 are shown in section a number of pieces one within the other, the central bore being filled with short plugs. All the cross-hatching was done with the triangle of 60 degrees and that of 90 degrees. It is here shown that with these two triangles only, and a judicious arrangement of the diagonals, an almost infinite number of pieces may be shown in cross section without any liability of mistaking one for the other, or any doubt as to the form and arrangement of the pieces; for, beside the difference in spacing in the cross-hatching, there are no two adjoining pieces with the diagonals running in the same direction. It will be seen that the narrow pieces are most clearly defined by a close spacing of the cross-hatching.

Fig. 90.

In Figure 91 are shown three pieces put together and having slots or keyways through them. The outer shell is shown to be in one piece from end to end, because the cross-hatching is not only equally spaced, but the diagonals are in the same direction; hence it would be known that D, F, H, and E were slots or recesses through the piece. The same remarks apply to piece B, wherein G, J, K are recesses or slots. Piece C is shown to have in its bore a recess at L. In the case of B, as of A, there would be no question as to the piece being all one from end to end, notwithstanding that the two ends are completely severed where the slots G, I, come, because the spacing and direction of the cross-hatching are equal on each side of the slots, which they would not be if they were separate pieces.

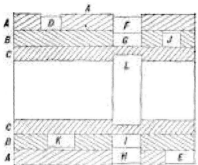 Fig. 91.

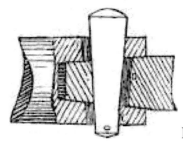 Fig. 92.

Section shading or cross-hatching may sometimes cause the lines of the drawing to appear crooked to the eye. Thus, in Figure 92, the key edge on the right appears curved inwards, while on the left the key edge appears curved outwards, although such is not actually the case. The same effect is produced in Figure 93 on the right-hand edge of the key, but not on the left-hand edge.

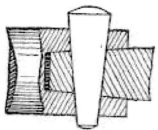 Fig. 93

Fig. 94.

A remarkable instance of this kind is shown in Figure 94, when the vertical lines appear to the eye to be at a considerable angle one to the other, although they are parallel.

The lines in sectional shading or cross-hatching may be made to denote the material of which the piece is to be composed. Thus Professor Unwin has proposed the system shown in the Figures 95 and 96. This may be of service in some cases, but it would involve very much more labor than it is worth in ordinary machine shop drawings, except in the case of cast iron and wood, these two being shown in the simplest and the usual manner. It is much better to write the name of the material beneath the piece in a detail drawing.

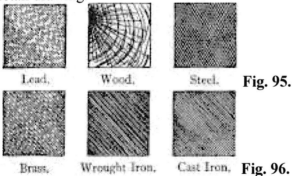

Lead.   Wood.   Steel.   **Fig. 95.**

Brass.   Wrought Iron.   Cast Iron.   **Fig. 96.**

LINE SHADING.

Mechanical drawings are made to look better and to show more distinctly by being line shaded or shaded by lines. The simplest form of line shading is by the use of the shade or shadow line.

In a mechanical drawing the light is supposed, for the purposes of line shading or of coloring, to come in from the upper left-hand corner of the drawing paper; hence it falls directly upon the upper and left-hand lines of each piece, which are therefore represented by fine lines, while the right hand and lower edges of the piece being on the shadow side may therefore, with propriety, be represented by broader lines, which are called shadow or shade lines. These lines will often serve to indicate the shape of some part of the piece represented, as will be seen from the following examples. In Figure 97 is a piece that contains a hole, the fact being shown by the circle being thickened at A. If the circle were thickened on the other side as at B, in Figure 98, it would show that it represented a cylindrical stem instead of a hole.

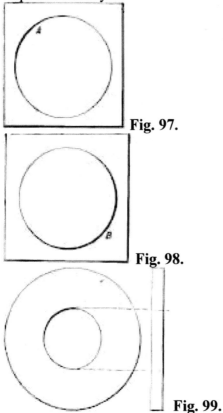

Fig. 97.

Fig. 98.

Fig. 99.

In Figure 99 is represented a washer, the surfaces that are in the shadow side being shown in a shade line or shadow line, as it is often called.

In Figure 100 is a key drawn with a shade line, while in Figure 101 the shade line is shown applied to a nut. The shade line may be produced in straight lines by drawing the line twice over, and slightly inclining the pen, or by opening the pen points a little. For circles, however, it may be produced either by slightly moving the centre from which the circle is drawn, or by going over the shade part twice, and slightly pressing the instrument as it moves, so as to gradually spring the legs farther apart, the latter plan being generally preferable.

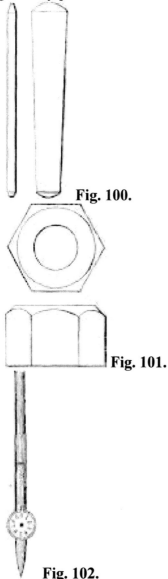

Fig. 100.

Fig. 101.

Fig. 102.

Figure 102 shows a German pen, that can be regulated to draw lines of various breadths. The head of the adjusting screw is made rather larger than usual, and is divided at the under side into twenty divisional notches, each alternate notch being marked by a figure on the face. By this arrangement a uniform thickness of line may be maintained after filling or clearing the pen, and any desired thickness may be repeated, without any loss of time in trial of thickness on the paper. A small spring automatically holds the divided screw-head in any place. With very little practice the click of the spring in the notches becomes a sufficient guide for adjustment, without reference to the figures on the screw-head. Another meritorious feature of this pen is that it is armed with sapphire points, which retain their sharpness very long, and thus save the time and labor required to keep ordinary instruments in order for the performance of fine work.

An example of line shading in perspective drawing is shown in the drawing of a pipe threading stock and die in Figure 103.

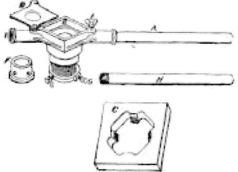

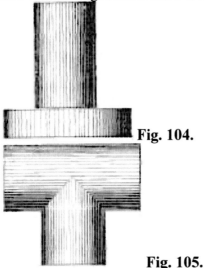

Fig. 103.

Shading by means of lines may be used with excellent effect in mechanical drawing, not only to distinguish round from flat surfaces, but also to denote to the eye the relative distances of surfaces. Figure 104 represents a cylindrical pin line shaded. As the light is supposed to come in from the upper left-hand corner, it will evidently fall more upon the left-hand half of the stem, and of the collar or bead, hence those parts are shaded with lighter or finer lines than the right-hand sides are.

Fig. 104.

Fig. 105.

Two cylindrical pieces that join each other may be line shaded at whatever angle they may join. Figure 105 represents two such pieces, one at a right angle to the other, both being of equal diameter.

Fig. 106.

Figure 106 represents a drawing of a lathe centre shaded by lines, the lines on the taper parts meeting those on the parallel part A, and becoming more nearly parallel to the axis of the piece as the centre of the piece is approached. The same is the case where a piece having a curved outline is drawn, which is shown in Figure 107, where the set of the bow-pen is gradually increased for drawing the shade lines of the curves. The centres of the shade curves fall in each case upon a line at a right angle to the axis of the piece, as upon the lines A, B, C, the dotted lines showing the radius for each curve.

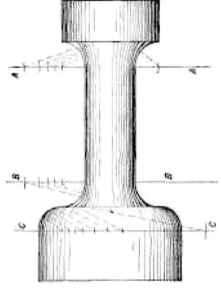

Fig. 107.

The lines are made finer by closing the pen points by means of the screw provided for that purpose. The pen requires for this purpose to be cleaned of the ink that is apt to dry in it.

In Figure 108 line shading is shown applied to a ball or sphere, while in Figure 109 it is shown applied to a pin in a socket which is shown in section. By showing the hollow in connection with the round piece, the difference between the two is quite clearly seen, the light falling most upon the upper half of the pin and the lower half of the hole. This perhaps is more clearly shown in the piece of tube in Figure 110, where the thickness of the tube showing is a great aid to the eye. So, likewise, the hollow or hole is more clearly seen where the piece is shown in section, as in Figure 111, which is the case even though the piece be taper as in the figure. If the body be bell-mouthed, as in Figure 112, the hollow curve is readily shown by the shading; but to line shade a hollow curve without any of these aids to the eye, as say, to show a half of a tin tube, is a very difficult matter if the piece is to look natural; and all that can be done is to shade the top darkly and let the light fall mostly at and near the bottom. An example of line shading to denote the relative distances from the eye of various surfaces is given in Figure 113, where the surfaces most distant are the most shaded. The flat surfaces are lined with lines of equal breadth, the degrees of shading being governed by the width apart of the lines.

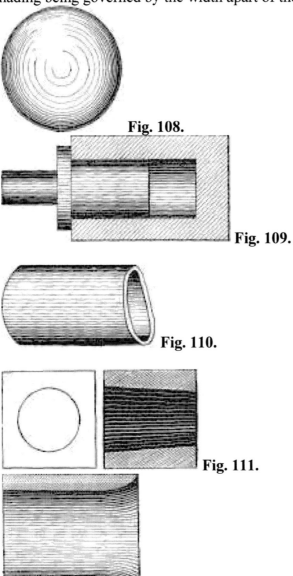

Fig. 108.

Fig. 109.

Fig. 110.

Fig. 111.

Fig. 112.

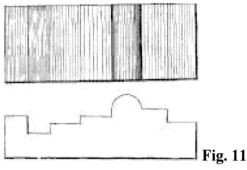

Fig. 113.

Line shading is often used to denote that the piece represented is to be of wood, the shade lines being in some cases regular in combination with regular ones, or entirely irregular, as in Figure 114.

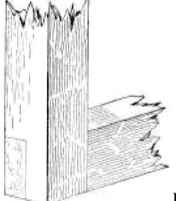

Fig. 114.

CHAPTER V.

MARKING DIMENSIONS.

The dimensions of mechanical drawings are best marked in red ink so that they will show plainly, and that the lines denoting the points at which the dimension is given shall not be confounded with the lines of the drawing.

The dimension figures should be as large as the drawing will conveniently admit; and should be marked at every point at which a shoulder or change of form or dimension occurs, except in the case of straight tapers which have their dimensions marked at each end of the taper.

In the case of a single piece standing by itself the dimension figures may be marked all standing one way, so as to be read without changing the position of the operator or requiring to turn the drawing around. This is done in Figure 115, which represents the drawing of a key. The figures are here placed outside the drawing in all cases where it can be done, which, in the case of a small drawing, leaves the same clearer.

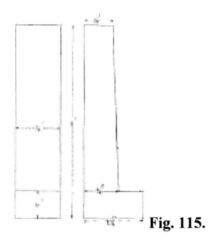

Fig. 115.

In Figure 116 the dimensions are marked, running parallel to the dimension for which they are given, so that all measures of length stand lengthwise, and those of breadth across the drawing.

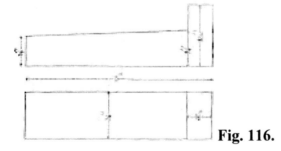

Fig. 116.

Figure 117 represents a key with a sharp-cornered step in it. Here the two dimensions forming the steps cannot both be coincident with it; hence they are marked as near to it as convenient, it being understood that they apply to the step, and not to one side of it. When the step has a round instead of a sharp corner, the radius of the arc of the corner may be marked, as shown in Figure 118.

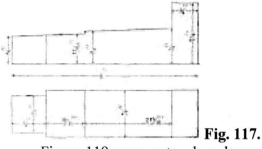

Fig. 117.

Figure 119 represents a key drawn in perspective, so that all the dimensions may be marked on one view. Perspective sketches may be used for single pieces, as they denote the shape of the piece more clearly to the eye. On account of the skill required in their production, they are not, however, used in mechanical drawing, except as in the case of Patent-Office or similar drawings, where the form and construction rather than the dimension is the information sought to be conveyed.

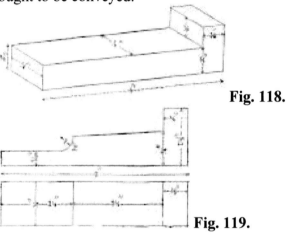

Fig. 118.

Fig. 119.

CHAPTER VI.

THE ARRANGEMENT OF DIFFERENT VIEWS.

THE DIFFERENT VIEWS OF A MECHANICAL DRAWING.

The word *elevation*, as applied to mechanical drawing, means simply a view; hence a side elevation is a side view, or an end elevation is an end view.

The word *plan* is employed in place of the word top; hence a plan view is a top view, or a view looking down upon the top of the piece.

A *general* view means a view showing the machine put together or assembled, while a detail drawing is one containing a detail, as a part of the machine or a single piece disconnected from the other parts of the whole machine.

It is obviously desirable in a mechanical drawing to present the piece of work in as few views as possible, but in all cases there must be a sufficient number to permit of the dimensions in every necessary direction to be marked on the drawing. Suppose, then, that in Figure 120 we have to represent a solid cylinder, whose length equals its diameter, and it is obvious that both the diameter and length may be marked in the one view given; hence, a second view, such as shown by the circle in Figure 121, is unnecessary, except it be to distinguish the body from a cube, in which the one view would also be sufficient whereon to mark all the dimensions necessary to enable the piece to be made. It happens, however, that a cube and a cylinder are the only two figures upon which all the dimensions can be marked on one view of the piece, and as cylindrical pieces are much more common in machine work than cubes are, it is taken for granted that, where the pieces are cylindrical, but one view shall be used, and that where they are cubes either two views shall be given, or where they are square a cross shall be marked upon the parts that are square; thus, in Figure 122, is shown a cross formed by the lines A B across the face of the drawing, which saves making a second view.

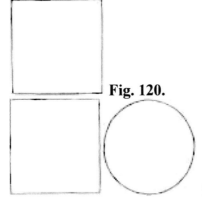

Fig. 120.

Fig. 121.

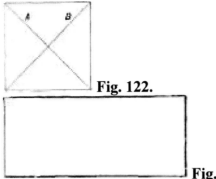

Fig. 122.

Fig. 123.

It would appear that under some conditions this might lead to error; as, for example, take the piece in Figure 123, and there is nothing to denote which is the length and which is the diameter of the piece, but there is a certain amount of custom in such cases than will usually determine this point; thus, the piece will be given a name, as pin or disk, the one denoting that its diameter is less than its length, and the other that its diameter is greater than its length. In the absence of any such name, it would be in practice assumed that it was a pin and not a disk; because, if it were a disk, it would either be named or shaded, or a second view given to show its unusual form, the disk being a more unusual form than the pin-form in mechanical structures. As an example of the use of the cross to denote a square, we have Figure 124, which represents a piece having a hexagon head, section a, a', that is rectangular, a collar b, a square part c, and a round stem d. Here it will be noted that it is the rectangular part a, a', that renders necessary two views, and that in the absence of the cross, yet another view would be necessary to show that part c is square.

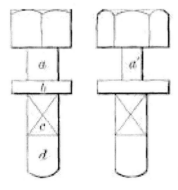

Fig. 124.

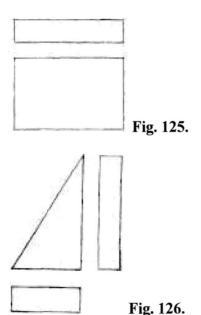

Fig. 125.

Fig. 126.

A rectangular piece always requires two views and sometimes three. In Figure 125, for example, is a piece that would require a side view to show the length and breadth, and an edge view to show the thickness. Suppose the piece to be wedge-shaped in any direction; then another view will be necessary, as is shown in Figs. 126 and 127. In the former the wedge or taper is in the direction of its length, while in the latter it is in the direction of its thickness. Outline views, however, will not in some cases show the form of the figure, however many views be presented. An example of this is given in Figure 128, which represents a ring having a hexagon cross section. A sectional edge view is here necessary in order to show the hexagonal form. Another example of this kind, which occurs more frequently in practice, is a cupped ring such as shown in Figure 129.

Fig. 127.

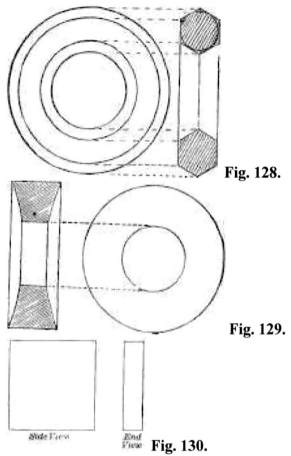

Fig. 128.

Fig. 129.

Side View   End View **Fig. 130.**

EXAMPLES.

Let it be required to draw a rectangular piece such as is shown in two views in Figure 130, and the process for the pencil lines is as follows:

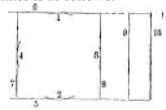

Fig. 131.

With the bow-pencil set to half the required length and breadth of the square the arcs 1, 2, 3 and 4, in Figure 131, are marked, and then the lines 5 and 6, letting them run past the width of the arcs 3 and 4. There is no need to pencil in lines 7 and 8, since they can be inked in without pencilling, because it is known that they must meet the arcs 3 and 4 and terminate at the lines 5 and 6. The top and bottom lines of the edge view are merely prolongations of lines 5 and 6; hence the lines 9 and 10 are drawn the requisite distance apart for the thickness and to meet the top and bottom lines. The lines are then inked in, the pencil lines rubbed out, and the drawing will appear as in Figure 130.

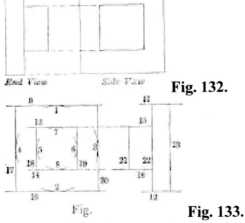

End View   Side View   **Fig. 132.**

Fig.   **Fig. 133.**

Suppose, however, that the piece has a step in it, as in Figure 132, and the pencilling will be as in Figure 133. From the centre, the arcs 1, 2, 3 and 4 for the outer, and arcs 5, 6, 7 and 8 for the inner square are marked; lines 9 and 10, and their prolongations, 11 and 12, for the edge view, are then pencilled; lines 13 and 14, and their prolongations, 15 and 16, are then pencilled, and dots to show the locations for lines 21 and 22 maybe marked and the pencilling is complete. Lines 17, 18, 19, 20, 21, 22, and 23 may then be inked in, in the order named, and then lines 9, 10, 11, 12, 13, 14, 15 and 16, when the inking in will be complete.

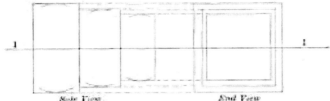

Side View   End View   **Fig. 134.**

In inking in horizontal lines begin at the top and mark in each line as the square comes to it; and in inking the vertical ones begin always at the left hand line and mark the lines as they are come to, moving the square or the triangle to the right, and great care should be taken not to let the lines cross where they meet, as at the corners, since this would greatly impair the appearance of the drawing.

These figures have been drawn without the aid of a centre line, because from their shapes it was easy to dispense with it, but in most cases a centre line is necessary; thus in Figure 134 we have a body having a number of steps. The diameters of these steps are marked by arcs, as in the previous examples, and their lengths may be marked by applying the measuring rule direct to the drawing paper and making the necessary pencil mark.

But it would be tedious to mark the successive steps true one with the other by measuring each step, because one step would require to be pencilled in before the next could be marked. To avoid this the centre line 1, Figure 134, is first marked, and the arcs for the steps are then marked as shown. Centre lines are also necessary to show the alignment of one part to another; thus in Figure 135 is a cube with a hole passing through it. The dotted lines in the side view show that the hole passes clear through the piece and is a parallel one, while the centre line, being central to the outline throughout the piece, shows that the hole is equidistant, all through, from the walls of the piece.

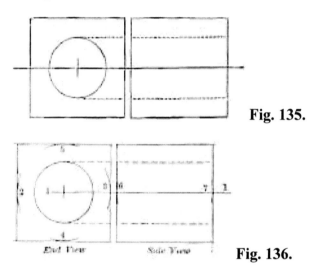

Fig. 135.

Fig. 136.

The pencil lines for this piece would be marked as in Figure 136, line 1 representing the centre line from which all the arcs are marked. It will be noted that the length of the piece is marked by arcs which occur, because being a cube the set of the compasses for arcs 2, 3, 4 and 5 will answer without altering to mark arcs 6 and 7.

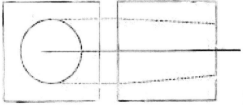

Fig. 137.

If the hole in the piece were a taper or conical one, it would be denoted by the dotted lines, as in Figure 137, and that the taper is central to the body is shown by these dotted lines being equidistant from the centre line.

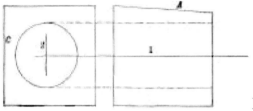

Fig. 138.

Suppose one of the sides to be tapered, as is the side A, in Figure 138, and that the hole is not central, and both facts will be shown by the centre lines 1 and 2 in the figure. The measurement of face A would be marked from A to line B at each end, but the distance the hole was out of the centre would be marked by the distance between the centre line 2 and the edge C of the piece.

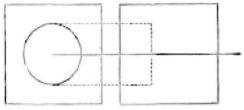

Fig. 139.

If the hole did not pass entirely through the piece, the dotted lines would show it, as in Figure 139.

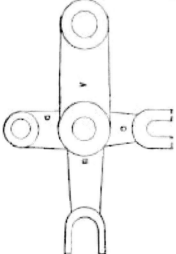

Fig. 140.

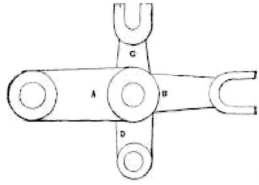

Fig. 141.

The designations of the views of a piece of work depend upon the position in which the piece stands, when in place upon the machine of which it forms a part. Thus in Figure 140 is a lever, and if its shaft stood horizontal when the piece is in place in the machine, the view given is an end one, but suppose that the shaft stood vertical, and the same view becomes a plan or top view.

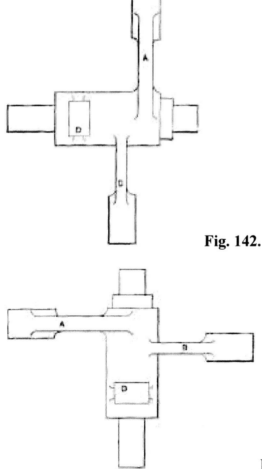

Fig. 142.

Fig. 143.

In Figure 142 is a view of a lever which is a side view if the lever stands horizontal, and lever B hangs down, or a plan view if the shaft stands horizontal, but lever B stands also horizontal. We may take the same drawing and turn it around on the paper as in Figure 143, and it becomes a side view if the shaft stands vertical, and a plan view if the shaft stands horizontal and arm D vertical above it.

In a side or an end view, the piece that projects highest in the drawing is highest when upon the machine; also in a side elevation the piece that is at the highest point in the drawing extends farthest upward when the piece is on the machine. But in a plan or top view the height of vertical pieces is not shown, as appears in the case of arm D in Figure 143.

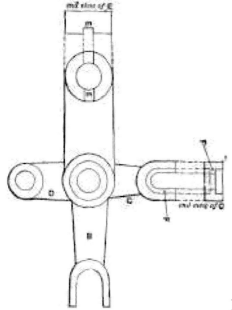

Fig. 144.

In either of the levers, Figures 142 or 143, all the dimensions could be marked if an additional view were given, but this will not be the case if an eye have a slot in it, as at E, in Figure 144, or a jaw have a tongue in it, as at F: hence, end views of the eye and the jaw must be given, which may be most conveniently done by showing them projected from the ends of those parts as in the figure.

This naturally brings us to a consideration as to the best method of projecting one view from another. As a general rule, the side elevation or side view is the most important, because it shows more of the parts and details of the work; hence it should be drawn first, because it affords more assistance in drawing the other views.

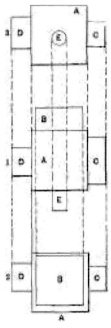

Fig. 145.

There are two systems of placing the different views of a piece. In the first the views are presented as the piece would present itself if it were laid upon the paper for the side view, and then turned or rolled upon the paper for the other views, as shown in Figure 145, in which the piece consists of five sections or members, marked respectively A, B, C, D, and E. Now if the piece were turned or rolled so that the end face of B were uppermost, and the member E was beneath, it will, by the operation of turning it, have assumed the position in the lower view marked position 2; while if it were turned over upon the paper in the opposite direction it would assume the position marked 3. This gives to the mind a clear idea of the various views and positions; but it possesses some disadvantages: thus, if position 1 is a side elevation or view of the piece, as it stands when in place of the machine, then E is naturally the bottom member; but it is shown in the top view of the drawing, hence what is actually the bottom view of the piece (position 3) becomes the top view in the drawing. A second disadvantage is that if we desire to put in dotted lines, to show how one view is derived from the other, and denote corresponding parts, then these dotted lines must be drawn across the face of the drawing, making it less distinct; thus the dotted lines connecting stem E in position 1 to E in position 3, pass across the faces of both A and B of position 1.

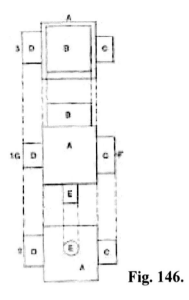

Fig. 146.

In a large drawing, or one composed of many members or parts, it would, therefore, be out of the question to mark in the dotted lines. A further disadvantage in a large drawing is that it is necessary to go from one side of the drawing to the other to see the construction of the same part.

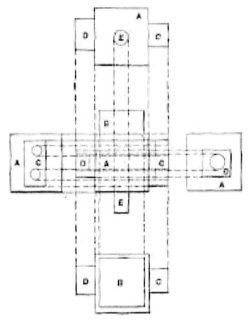

Fig. 147.

To obviate these difficulties, a modern method is to suppose the piece, instead of rolling upon the paper, to be lifted from it, turned around to present the required view, and then moved upwards on the paper for a top view, sideways for a side view, and below for a bottom view. Thus the three views of the piece in Figure 145 would be as in Figure 146, where position 2 is obtained by supposing the piece to be lifted from position 1, the bottom face turned uppermost, and the piece moved down the paper to position 2, which is a bottom view of the piece, and the bottom view in the drawing. Similarly, if the piece be lifted from position 1, and the top face in that figure is turned uppermost, and the piece is then slid upwards on the paper, view 3 is obtained, being a top view of the piece as it lies in position 1, and the top view in the drawing. Now suppose we require to find the shape of member B, then in Figure 145 we require to look at the top of position 1, and then down below to position 2.

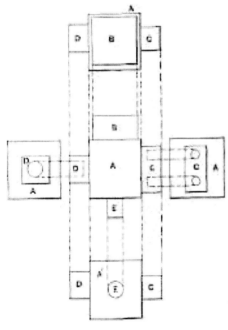

Fig. 148.

But in Figure 146 we have the side view and end view both together, while the dotted lines do not require to cross the face of the side view. Now suppose we take a similar piece, and suppose its end faces, as F, G, to have holes in them, which require to be shown in both views, and under the one system the drawing would, if the dotted lines were drawn across, appear as in Figure 147, whereas under the other system the drawing would appear as in Figure 148. And it follows that in cases where it is necessary to draw dotted lines from one view to the other, it is best to adopt the new system.

CHAPTER VII.

EXAMPLES IN BOLTS, NUTS, AND POLYGONS.

Fig. 149.

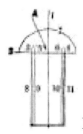

Fig. 150.

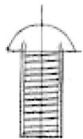

Fig. 151.

Let it be required to draw a machine screw, and it is not necessary, and therefore not usual in small screws to draw the full outline of the thread, but to represent it by thick and thin lines running diagonally across the bolt, as in Figure 149, the thick ones representing the bottom, and the thin ones the top of the thread. The pencil lines would be drawn in the order shown in Figure 150. Line 1 is the centre line, and line 2 a line to represent the lower side of the head; from the intersection of these two lines as a centre (as at A) short arcs 3 and 6, showing the diameter of the thread, are marked, and the arcs 5 and 6, representing the depth of the thread, are marked. The arc 7, representing the head, is then marked. The vertical lines 8, 9, 10, and 11 are then marked, and the outline of the screw is complete. The thick lines representing the bottom of the thread are next marked in, as in Figure 151, extending from line 9 to line 10. Midway between these lines fine ones are made for the tops of the thread. All the lines being pencilled in, they may be inked in with the drawing instruments, taking care that they do not overrun one another. When the pencil lines are rubbed out, the sketch will appear as in Figure 149.

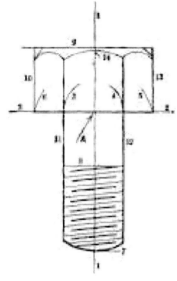

Fig. 152.

For a bolt with a hexagon head the lines would be drawn in the order shown in Figure 152. At a right-angle to centre line 1, line two is drawn. The pencil-compasses are then set to half the diameter of the bolt, and from point A arcs 3 and 6 are pencilled, thus showing the width of the front flat of the head, as well as the diameter of the stem. From the point where these arcs meet line 2, and with the same radius, arcs 5 and 6 are marked, showing the widths of the other two flats of the head. The thickness of the head and the length of the bolt head may then be marked either by placing a rule on line 1 and marking the short lines (such as line 7) a cross line 1, or the pencil-compasses may be set to the rule and the lengths marked from point A. In the United States standard for bolt heads and nuts the thickness of the head is made equal to the diameter of the bolt. With the compasses set for the arcs 3 and 4, we may in two steps, from A along the centre line, mark off the thickness of the head without using the rule. But as the rule has to be applied along line 1 to mark line 7 for the length of the bolt, it is just as easy to mark the head thickness at the same time. The line 8 showing the length of the thread may be marked at the same time as the other lengths are marked, and the outlines 9, 10, 11, 12, 13 may be drawn in the order named. We have now to mark the arcs at the top of the flats of the head to show the chamfer, and to explain how these arcs are obtained we have in Figure 153 an enlarged view of the head. It is evident that the smallest diameter of the chamfer is represented by the circle A, and therefore the length of the line B must equal A. It is also evident that the outer edge of the chamfer will meet the corners at an equal depth (from the face of the nut), as represented by the line C C, and it is obvious that the curves that represent the outline of the chamfer on each side of the head or nut will approach the face of the head or nut at an equal distance, as denoted by the line D D. It follows that the curve must in each case be such as will, at each of its ends, meet the line C, and at its centre meet the line D D, the centres of the respective curves being marked in the figure by X.

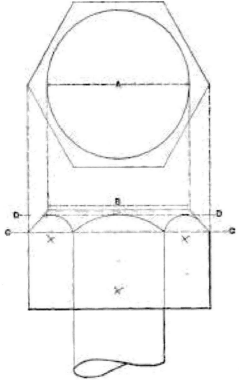

Fig. 153.

It is sufficiently accurate, therefore, for all practical purposes to set the pencil on the centre-line at the point A in Figure 152 and mark the curve 14, and to then set the compasses by trial to mark the other two curves of the chamfer, so that they shall be an equal distance with arc 14 from line 9, and join lines 10 and 13 at the same distance from line 9 that 14 joins lines 3 and 4, so that as in Figure 153 all three of the arcs would touch a line as C, and another line as D.

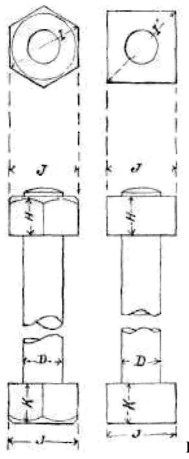

Fig. 154.

The United States standard sizes for forged or unfinished bolts and nuts are given in the following table, Figure 154 showing the dimensions referred to in the table.

UNITED STATES STANDARD DIMENSIONS OF BOLTS AND NUTS.

Bolt. Bolt Head and Nut. Diameter. Standard Number of threads per inch Long diameter, I, or diameter across corners Short diameter of hexagon and square, or width across J Depth of Nut, H Depth of bolt head, K Nominal. D. Effective. * Hexagon Square 1/4 .185 20 9/16 23/32 1/2 1/4 1/4 5/16 .240 18 11/16 27/32 19/32 5/16 19/64 3/8 .294 16 25/32 31/32 11/16 3/8 11/32 7/16 .345 14 29/32 1-3/32 25/32 7/16 25/64 1/2 .400 13 1 1-1/4 7/8 1/2 7/16 9/16 .454 12 1-1/8 1-3/8 31/32 9/16 31/64 5/8 .507 11 1-7/32 1-1/2 1-1/16 5/8 17/32 3/4 .620 10 1-7/16 1-3/4 1-1/4 3/4 5/8 7/8 .731 9 1-21/32 2-1/32 1-7/16 7/8 23/32 1 .837 8 1-7/8 2-5/16 1-5/8 1 13/16 1-1/8 .940 7 2-3/32 2-9/16 1-13/16 1-1/8 29/32 1-1/4 1.065 7 2-5/16 2-27/32 2 1-1/4 1 1-3/8 1.160 6 2-17/32 3-3/32 2-3/16& 1-3/8 1-3/32 1-1/2 1.284 6 2-3/4 3-11/32 2-3/8 1-1/2 1-3/16 1-5/8 1.389 5-1/2 2-31/32 3-5/8 2-9/16 1-5/8 1-9/32 1-3/4 1.491 5 3-3/16 3-7/8 2-3/4 1-3/4 1-3/8 1-7/8 1.616 5 3-13/32 4-5/32 2-15/16 1-7/8 1-15/32 2 1.712 4-1/2 3-19/32 4-13/32 3-1/8 2 1-9/16 2-1/4 1.962 4-1/2 4-1/32 4-15/16 3-1/2 2-1/4 1-3/4 2-1/2 2.176 4 4-15/32 5-15/32 3-7/8 2-1/2 1-15/16 2-3/4 2.426 4 4-29/32 6 4-1/4 2-3/4 2-1/8 3 2.629 3-1/2 5-11/32 6-17/32 4-5/8 3 2-5/16 3-1/4 2.879 3-1/2 5-25/32 7-1/16 5 3-1/4 2-1/2 3-1/2 3.100 3-1/4 6-7/32 7-19/32 5-3/8 3-1/2 2-11/16 3-3/4 3.317 3 6-5/8 8-1/8 5-3/4& 3-3/4 2-7/8 ... 3.567 3 7-1/16 8-21/32 6-1/8 3-1/16 4-1/4 3.798 2-7/8 7-1/2 9-3/16 6-1/2 4-1/4 3-1/4 4-1/2 4.028 2-3/4 7-15/16 9-23/32 6-7/8 4-1/2 3-7/16 4-3/4 4.256 2-5/8 8-3/8 10-1/4 7-1/4 4-3/4 3-5/8 5 4.480 2-1/2 8-13/16 10-25/32 7-5/8 5 3-13/16 5-1/4 4.730 2-1/2 9-1/4 11-5/16 8 5-1/4 4 5-1/2 4.953 2-3/8 9-11/16 11-27/32 8-3/8 5-1/2 4-3/16 5-3/4 5.203 2-3/8 10-3/32 12-3/8 8-3/4 5-3/4 4-3/8 6 5.423 2-1/4 10-17/32 12-29/32 9-1/8 6 4-9/16
* Diameter at the root of the thread.

The basis of the Franklin Institute or United States standard for the heads of bolts and for nuts is as follows:
The short diameter or width across the flats is equal to one and one-half times the diameter plus 1/8 inch for rough or unfinished bolts and nuts, and one and one-half times the bolt diameter plus, 1/16 inch for finished heads and nuts. The thickness is, for rough heads and nuts, equal to the diameter of the bolt, and for finished heads and nuts 1/16 inch less.

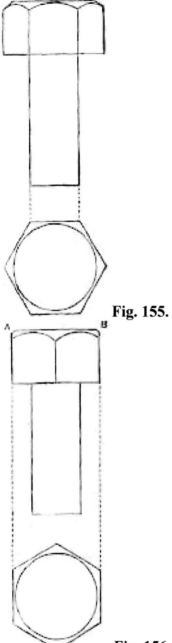

Fig. 155.

Fig. 156.

The hexagonal or hexagon (as they are termed in the shop) heads of bolts may be presented in two ways, as is shown in Figures 155 and 156.

The latter is preferable, inasmuch as it shows the width across the flats, which is the dimension that is worked to, because it is where the wrench fits, and therefore of most importance; whereas the latter gives the length of a flat, which is not worked to, except incidentally, as it were. There is the objection to the view of the head, given in Figure 156, however, that unless it is accompanied by an end view it somewhat resembles a similar view of a square head for a bolt. It may be distinguished therefrom, however, in the following points:

If the amount of chamfer is such as to leave the chamfer circle (as circle A, in Figure 153) of smaller diameter than the width across the flats of the bolt-head, the outline of the sides of the head will pass above the arcs at the top of the flats, and there will be two small flat places, as A and B, in Figure 156 (representing the angle of the chamfer), which will not meet the arcs at the top of the flats, but will join the sides above those arcs, as in the figure; which is also the case in a similar view of a square-headed bolt. It may be distinguished therefrom, however, in the following points:

If the amount of chamfer is such as to leave the chamfer circle (A, Figure 153) of smaller diameter than the width across the flats of the bolt-head, the outline of the sides will pass above the arc on the flats, as is shown in Figure 157, in which the chamfer A meets the side of the head at B, and does not, therefore, meet the arc C. The length of side lying between B and D in the side view corresponds with the part lying between E and F in the end view.

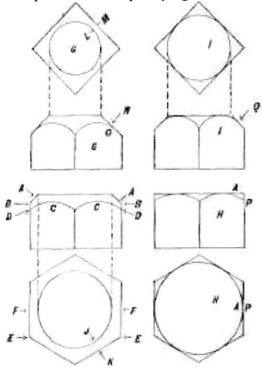

Fig. 157.

If we compare this head with similar views of a square head G, both being of equal widths, and having their chamfer circles at an equal distance from the sides of the flats, and at the same angle, we perceive at once that the amount of chamfer necessary to give the same distance between the chamfer circle and the side of the bolt (that is, the distance from J to K, being equal to that from L to M), the length of the chamfer N for the square head so greatly exceeds the length A for the hexagon head that the eye detects the difference at once, and is instinctively informed that G must be square, independently of the fact that in the case of the square head, N meets the arc O, while in the hexagon head, A, which corresponds to N, does not meet the arc C, which corresponds to O.

When, however, the chamfer is drawn, but just sufficient to meet the flats, as in the case of the hexagon H, and the square I, in Figure 157, the chamfer line passes from the chamfer circle to the side of the head, and the distinction is greater, as will be seen by comparing head H with head I, both being of equal width, having the same angle of chamfer, and an amount just sufficient to meet the sides of the flats. Here it will be seen that in the hexagon H, each side of the head, as P, meets the chamfer circle A. Whereas, in the square head these two lines are joined by the chamfer line Q, the figures being quite dissimilar.

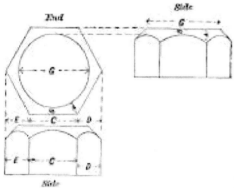

Fig. 158.

It is obvious that whatever the degree or angle of the chamfer may be, the diameter of the chamfer circle will be the same in any view in which the head may be presented. Thus, in Figure 158, the line G in the side view is in length equal to the diameter of circle G, in the end view, and so long as the angle of the chamfer is forty-five degrees, as in all the views hitherto given, the width of the chamfer will be equal at corresponding points in the different views;

thus in the figure the widths A and B in the two views are equal.

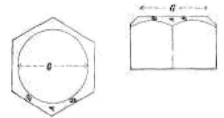

Fig. 159.

If the other view showing a corner of the head in front of the head be given, the same fact holds good, as is shown in Figure 159. That the two outside flats should appear in the drawing to be half the width of the middle flat is also shown in Figure 158, where D and E are each half the width of C. Let us now suppose, that the chamfer be given some other angle than that of 45 degrees, and we shall find that the effect is to alter the curves of the chamfer arcs on the flats, as is shown in Figure 160, where these arcs E, C, D are shown less curved, because the chamfer B has more angle to the flats. As a result, the width or distance between the arcs and line G is different in the two views. On this account it is better to draw the chamfer at 45 degrees, as correct results may be obtained with the least trouble.

If no chamfer at all is to be given, a hexagon head may still be distinguished from a square one, providing that the view giving three sides of the head, as in Figure 158, is shown, because the two sides D and E being half the width of the middle one C, imparts the information that it is a hexagon head. If, however, the view showing but two of the sides and a corner in front is given, and no chamfer is used, it could not be known whether the head was to be hexagon or square, unless an end view be given, as in Figure 161.

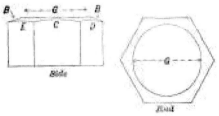

Fig. 160.

If the view showing a full side of the head of a square-headed bolt is given, then either an end view must be given, as in Figure 162, or else a single view with a cross on its head, as in

Figure 163, may be given.

It is the better plan, both in square and hexagon heads, to give the view in which the full face of a flat is presented, that is, as in Figures 155 and 163; because, in the case of the square, the length of a side and the width across the head are both given in that view; whereas if two sides are shown, as in Figure 161, the width across flats is not given, and this is the dimension that is wanted to work to, and not the width across corners. In the case of a hexagon the middle of the three flats is equal in width to the diameter of the bolt, and the other two are one-half its width; all three, therefore, being marked with the same set of compasses as gives the diameter of the body of the bolt, were as shown in Figure 152. For the width across flats there is an accepted standard; hence there is no need to mark it upon the drawing, unless in cases where the standard is to be departed from, in which event an end view may be added, or the view showing two sides may be given.

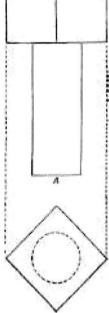

Fig 161.

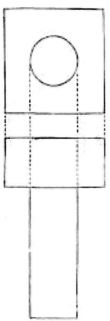

Fig. 162.

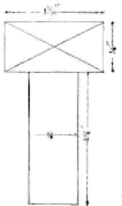

Fig. 163.

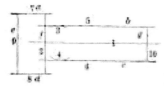

Fig. 164.

To draw a square-headed bolt, the pencil lines are marked in the order shown by figures in Figure 164. The inking in is done in the order of the letters *a*, *b*, *c*, etc. It will be observed that pencil lines 2, 9, and 10 are not drawn to cross, but only to meet the lines at their ends, a point that, as before stated, should always be carefully attended to.

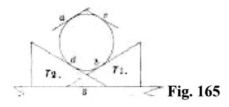

Fig. 165

To draw the end view of a hexagon head, first draw a circle of the diameter across the flats, and then rest the triangle of 60 degrees on the blade *s* of the square, as at T 1, in Figure 165, and mark the lines *a* and *b*. Reverse the triangle, as at T 2, and draw lines *c* and *d*. Then place the triangle as in Figure 166, and draw the lines *e* and *f*.

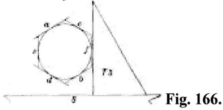

Fig. 166.

If the other view of the head is to be drawn, then first draw the lines *a* and *b* in Figure 167 with the square, then with the 60 degree triangle, placed on the square S, as at T 1, draw the lines *c*, *d*, and turning the square over, as at T 2, mark lines *e* and *f*.

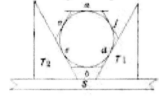

Fig. 167.

If the diameter across corners of a square head is given, and it be required to draw the head, the process is as follows: For a view showing one corner in front, as in Figure 168, a circle of the given diameter across corners is pencilled, and the horizontal centre-line *a* is marked, and the triangle of 45 degrees is rested against the square blade S, as in position T 1, and lines *b* and *c* marked, *b* being marked first; and the triangle is then slid along the square blade to position T 1, when line *c* is marked, these two lines just meeting the horizontal line *a*, where it meets the circle. The triangle is then moved to the left, and line *d*, joining the ends of *b* and *c*, is marked, and by moving it still farther to the left to position T 2, line *e* is marked. Lines *b*, *c*, *d*, and *e* are, of course, the only ones inked in.

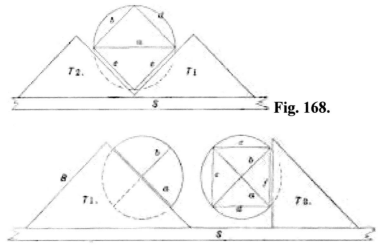

Fig. 168.

Fig.

169.

If the flats are to lie in the other direction, the pencilling will be done as in Figure 169. The circle is marked as before, and with the triangle placed as shown at T 1, line *a*, passing through the centre of the circle, is drawn. By moving the triangle to the right its edge B will be brought into position to mark line *b*, also passing through the centre of the circle. All that remains is to join the ends of these two lines, using the square blade for lines *c*, *d*, and the triangle for *e* and *f*, its position on the square blade being denoted at T 3; lines *c*, *d*, *e*, *f*, are the ones inked in.

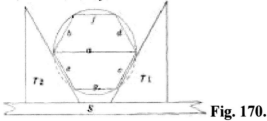

Fig. 170.

For a hexagon head we have the processes, Figures 170 and 171. The circle is struck, and across it line *a*, Figure 170, passing through its centre, the triangle of sixty degrees will mark the sides *b*, *c*, and *d*, *e*, as shown, and the square blade is used for *f*, *g*.

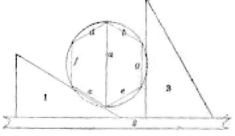

Fig. 171.

The chamfer circles are left out of these figures to reduce the number of lines and so keep the engraving clear. Figure 171 shows the method of drawing a hexagon head when the diameter across corners is given, the lines being drawn in the alphabetical order marked, and the triangle used as will now be understood.

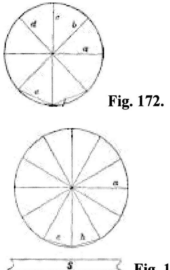

Fig. 172.

Fig. 173.

It may now be pointed out that the triangle may be used to divide circles much more quickly than they could be divided by stepping around them with compasses. Suppose, for example, that we require to divide a circle into eight equal parts, and we may do so as in Figure 172, line *a* being marked from the square, and lines *b*, *c* and *d* from the triangle of forty-five degrees; the lines to be inked in to form an octagon need not be pencilled, as their location is clearly defined, being lines joining the ends of the lines crossing the circle, as for example, lines *e*, *f*.

Let it be required to draw a polygon having twelve equal sides, and the triangle of sixty is used, marking all the lines within the circle in Figure 173, except *a*, for which the square blade is used; the only lines to be inked in are such as *b*, *c*. In this example there is a corner at the top and bottom, but suppose it were required that a flat should fall there instead of a corner; then all we have to do is to set the square blade S at the required angle, as in Figure 174, and then proceed as before, bearing in mind that the point of the circle nearest to the square blade, straight-edge, or whatever the triangle is rested on, is always a corner of a polygon having twelve sides.

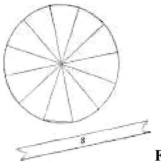

Fig. 174.

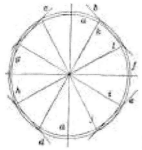

Fig. 175.

In both of these examples we have assumed that the diameter across corners of the polygon was given, but suppose the diameter across the flats were given, and the construction is a little more complicated. Circle *a*, *a*, in Figure 175, is drawn of the required diameter across the flats, and the lines of division are drawn across with the triangle of 60 as before; the triangle of 45 is then used to draw the four lines, *b*, *c*, *d*, *e*, joining the ends of lines *i*, *j*, *k*, *l*, and touching the inner circle, *a*, *a*. The outer circle is then pencilled in, touching the lines of division where they meet the lines *b*, *c*, *d*, *e*, and the rest of the lines for the sides of the polygon may then be drawn within the outer circle, as at *g*, *h*.

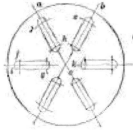

Fig. 176.

It is obvious, also, that the triangle may be used to draw slots radiating from a centre, as in Figure 176, where it is desired to draw a chuck-plate having 6 slots. The triangle of 60 is used to draw the centre lines, *a*, *b*, *c*, etc., for the slots. From the centre, the arcs *e*, *f*, *g*, *h*, etc., are marked, showing where the centres will fall for describing the half circles forming the ends of the slots. Then half circles, *i, j, k, l*, etc., being drawn, the sides of the slots may be drawn in with the triangle, and the outer circle and the slots inked in.

If the slots are not to radiate from the centre of the circle the process is as follows:

The outer circle *a*, Figure 177, being drawn, an inner one *b* is drawn, its radius equalling the amount; the centres of the slots are to point to one side of the centre of circle *a*. The triangle is then used to divide the circle into the requisite number of divisions *c* for the slots, and arcs *i, j*, are then drawn for the lengths of the slots. The centre lines *e* are then drawn, passing through the lines *c*, and the arcs *i, j*, etc., and touching the perimeter of the inner circle *b*; arcs *f, g*, are then marked in, and their sides joined with the triangle adjusted by hand. All that would be inked in black are the outer circle and the slots, but the inner circle *b* and a centre line of one of the slots should be marked in red ink to show how the inclination of the slot was obtained, and therefore its amount.

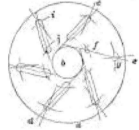

Fig. 177.

For a five-sided figure it is best to step around the circumference of the circle with the compasses, but for a three-sided one, or trigon, the construction is as follows: It will be found that the compasses set to the radius of a circle will accurately divide it into six equal divisions, as is shown in Figure 178; hence every other one of these divisions will be the location for a corner of a trigon.

The circle being drawn, a line A, 179, is drawn through its centre, and from its intersection with the circle as at *b*, here a step on each side is marked as *c, d*, then lines *c* to *d*, and *c* and *d* to *e*, where A meets, the circle will describe a trigon. If the figure is to stand vertical, all that is necessary is to draw the line *a* vertical, as in Figure 180. A ready method of getting the dimension across corners, across the flats, or the length of a side of a given polygon, is by means of diagrams, such as shown in the following figures, which form excellent examples for practice.

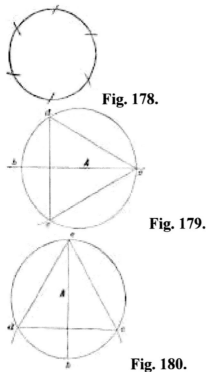

Fig. 178.

Fig. 179.

Fig. 180.

Draw the line O P, Figure 181, and at a right angle to it the line O B; divide these two lines into parts of one inch, as shown in the cut, which is divided into inches and quarter inches, and from these points of division draw lines crossing each other as shown.

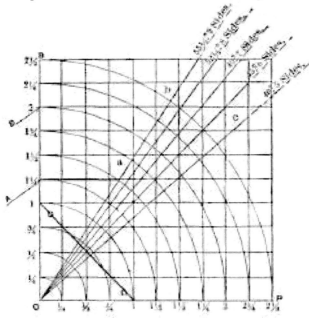

Fig. 181.

From the point O, draw diagonal lines, at suitable angles to the line O P. As shown in the cut, these diagonal lines are marked:

40 degrees for 5 sided figures. 45 " " 6 " " 49 " " 7 " " 52-1/2 " " 8 " " 55-1/2 " " 9 " "

But still others could be added for figures having a greater number of sides.

1. Now it will be found as follows: Half the diameter, or the radius of a piece of cylindrical work being given, and the number of sides it is to have being stated, the length of one side will be the distance measured horizontally from the line O B to the diagonal line for that particular number of sides.

Example.—A piece of work is 2-1/2 inches in diameter, and is required to have 9 sides: what will be the length of the sides or flats?

Now the half diameter or radius of 2-1/2 inches is 1-1/4 inches. Then look along the line O B for 1-1/4, which is denoted in the cut by figures and the arrow A; set one point of the compasses at A, and the other at the point of crossing of the diagonal line with the 1-1/4 horizontal line, as shown in the figure at *a*, and from A to *a* is the length of one side.

Again: A piece of work, 4 inches in diameter, is to have 9 sides: how long will each side be?

Now half of 4 is 2, hence from B to *b* is the length of each side.

But suppose that from the length of each side, and the number of sides, it is required to find the diameter to which to turn the piece; that is, its diameter across corners, and we simply reverse the process thus: A body has 9 sides, each side measures 27/32: what is its diameter across corners?

Take a rule, apply it horizontally on the figure, and pass it along till the distance from the line O B to the diagonal line marked 9 sides measures 27/32, which is from 1-1/4 on O B to *a*, and the 1-1/4 is the radius, which, multiplied by 2, gives 2-1/2 inches, which is the required diameter across corners.

For any other number of sides the process is just the same. Thus: A body is 3-1/2 inches in diameter, and is to have 5 sides: what will be the length of each side? Now half of 3-1/2 is 1-3/4; hence from 1-3/4 on the line O B to the point C, where the diagonal line crosses the 1-3/4 line, is the length of each of the sides.

2. It will be found that the length of a side of a square being given, the size of the square, measured across corners, will be the length of the diagonal line marked 45 degrees, from the point O to the figures indicating, on the line O B or on the line O P, the length

of one side.

Example.—A square body measures 1 inch on each side: what does it measure across the corners? Answer: From the point O, along diagonal line marked 45 degrees, to the point where it crosses the lines 1 (as denoted in the figure by a dot).

Again: A cylindrical piece of wood requires to be squared, and each side of the square must measure an inch: what diameter must the piece be turned to?

Now the diagonal line marked 45 degrees passes through the 1-inch line on O B, and the inch line on O P, at the point where these lines meet; hence all we have to do is to run the eye along either of the lines marked inch, and from its point of meeting the 45 degrees line, to the point O, is the diameter to turn the piece to.

There is another way, however, of getting this same measurement, which is to set a pair of compasses from the line 1 on O B, to line 1 on O P, as shown by the line D, which is the full diameter across corners. This is apparent, because from point O, along line O B, to 1, thence to the dot, thence down to line 1 on O P, and along that to O, encloses a square, of which either from O to the dot, or the length of the line D, is the measurement across corners, while the length of each side, or diameter across the flats, is from point O to either of the points 1, or from either of the points 1 to the dot.

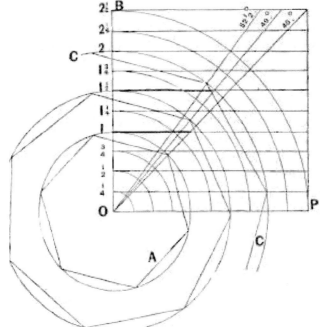

Fig. 182.

After graphically demonstrating the correctness of the scale we may simplify it considerably. In Figure 182, therefore, we have applications shown. A is a hexagon, and if one of its sides be measured, it will be found that it measures the same as along line 1 from O B to the diagonal line 45 degrees, which distance is shown by a thickened line.

At 1-1/2 is shown a seven-sided figure, whose diameter is 3 inches, and radius 1-1/2 inches, and if from the point at 1-1/2 (along the thickened horizontal line), to the diagonal marked 49 degrees, be measured, it will be found exactly equal to the length of a side on the polygon.

At C is shown part of a nine-sided polygon, of 2-inch radius, and the length of one of its sides will be found to equal the distance from the diagonal line marked 52-1/2 degrees, and the line O B at 2.

Let it now be noted that if from the point O, as a centre, we describe arcs of circles from the points of division on O B to O P, one end of each arc will meet the same figure on O P as it started from at O B, as is shown in Figure 181, and it becomes apparent that in the length of diagonal line between O and the required arc we have the radius of the polygon.

Example.—What is the radius across corners of a hexagon or six-sided figure, the length of a side being an inch?

Turning to our scale we find that the place where there is a horizontal distance of an inch between the diagonal 45 degrees, answering to six-sided figures, is along line 1 (Figure 182), and the radius of the circle enclosing the six-sided body is, therefore, an inch, as will be seen on referring to circle A. But it will be noted that the length of diagonal line 45 degrees, enclosed between the point O and the arc of circle from 1 on O B to one on O P, measures also an inch. Hence we may measure the radius along the diagonal lines if we choose. This, however, simply serves to demonstrate the correctness of the scale, which, being understood, we may dispense with most of the lines, arriving at a scale such as shown in Figure 183, in which the length of the side of the polygon is the distance from the line O B, measured horizontally to the diagonal, corresponding to the number of sides of the polygon. The radius across corners of the polygon is that of the distance from O along O B to the horizontal line, giving the length of the side of the polygon, and the width across corners for a given length of one side of the square, is measured by the length of the lines A, B, C, etc. Thus, dotted line 2 shows the length of the side of a nine-sided figure, of 2-inch radius, the radius across corners of the figure being 2 inches.

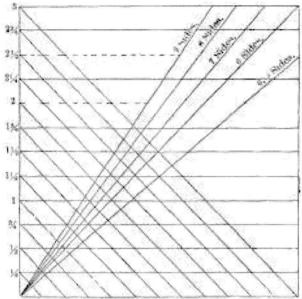

Fig. 183.

The dotted line 2-1/2 shows the length of the side of a nine-sided polygon, having a radius across corners of 2-1/2 inches. The dotted line 1 shows the diameter, across corners, of a square whose sides measure an inch, and so on.

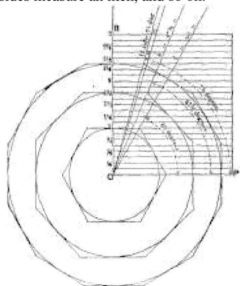

Fig. 184.

This scale lacks, however, one element, in that the diameter across the flats of a regular polygon being given, it will not give the diameter across the corners. This, however, we may obtain by a somewhat similar construction. Thus, in Figure 184, draw the line O B, and divide it into inches and parts of an inch. From these points of division draw horizontal lines; from the point O draw the

following lines and at the following angles from the horizontal line
O P.

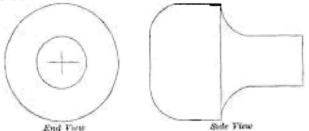

End View   Side View   **Fig. 185.**

A line at 75° for polygons having 12 sides.
"   72°   "   "   10 "
"   67-1/2° "   "   8 "
"   60°   "   "   6 "

From the point O to the numerals denoting the radius of the
polygon is the radius across the flats, while from point O to the
horizontal line drawn from those numerals is the radius across
corners of the polygon.

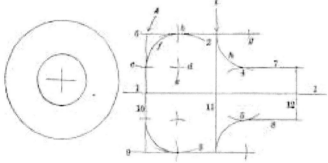

Fig. 186.

A hexagon measures two inches across the flats: what is its
diameter measured across the corners? Now from point O to the
horizontal line marked 1 inch, measured along the line of 60
degrees, is 1 5-32nds inches: hence the hexagon measures twice
that, or 2 5-16ths inches across corners. The proof of the
construction is shown in the figure, the hexagon and other polygons
being marked simply for clearness of illustration.

Fig. 187.

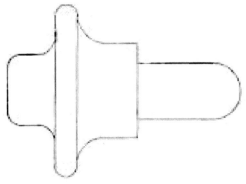

Fig. 188.

Let it be required to draw the stud shown in Figure 185, and the construction would be, for the pencil lines, as shown in Figure 186; line 1 is the centre line, arcs, 2 and 3 give the large, and arcs 4 and 5 the small diameter, to touch which lines 6, 7, 8, and 9 may be drawn. Lines 10, 11, and 12 are then drawn for the lengths, and it remains to draw the curves in. In drawing these curves great exactitude is required to properly find their centres; nothing looks worse in a drawing than an unfair or uneven junction between curves and straight lines. To find the location for these centres, set the compasses to the required radius for the curve, and from the point or corner A draw the arcs *b* and *c*, from *c* mark the arc *e*, and from *b* the arc *d*, and where *d* and *e* cross is the centre for the curve *f*.

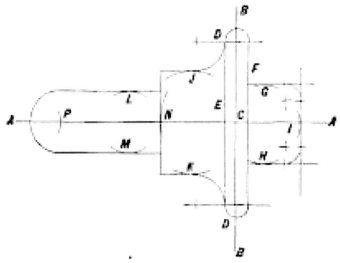

Fig. 189.

Similarly for the curve *h*, set the compasses on *i* and mark the arc *g*, and from the point where it crosses line 6, draw the curve *h*. In inking in it is best to draw in all curves or arcs of circles first, and the straight lines that join them afterward, because, if the straight lines are drawn first, it is a difficult matter to alter the centres of the curves to make them fall true, whereas, after the curves are drawn it is an easy matter, if it should be necessary, to vary the line a trifle, so as to make it join the curves correctly and fair. In inking in these curves also, care must be taken not to draw them too short or too long, as this would impair the appearance very much, as is shown in Figure 187.

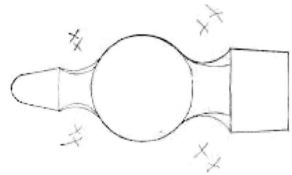

Fig. 190.

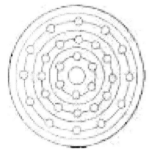

Fig. 191.

To draw the piece shown in Figure 188, the lines are drawn in the order indicated by the letters in Figure 189, the example being given for practice. It is well for the beginner to draw examples of common objects, such as the hand hammer in Figure 190, or the chuck plate in Figure 191, which afford good examples in the drawing of arcs and circles.

In Figure 191 *a* is a cap nut, and the order in which the same would be pencilled in is indicated by the respective numerals. The circles 3 and 4 represent the thread.

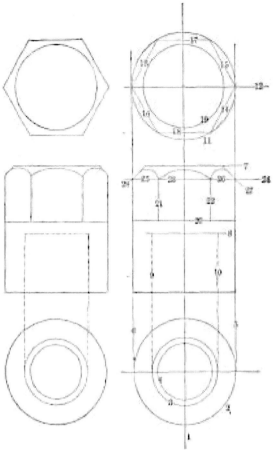

Fig. 191 a.

In Figure 192 is shown the pencilling for a link having the hubs on one side only, so that a centre line is unnecessary on the edge view, as all the lengths are derived from the top view, while the thickness of the stem and height of the hubs may be measured from the line A. In Figure 193 there are hubs (on both sides of the link) of unequal height, hence a centre line is necessary in both views, and from this line all measurements should be marked.

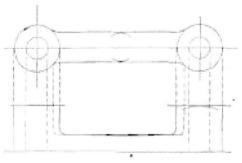

Fig. 192.

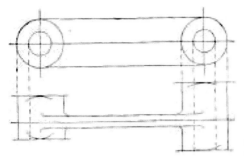

Fig. 193.

In Figure 194 are represented the pencil lines for a double eye or knuckle joint, as it is sometimes termed, an example that it is desirable for the student to draw in various sizes, as it is representative of a large class of work.

These eyes often have an offset, and an example of this is given in Figure 195, in which A is the centre line for the stem distant from the centre line B of the eyes to the amount of offset required.

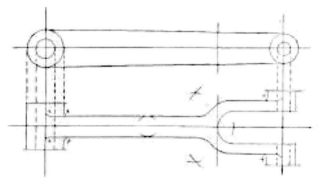

Fig. 194.

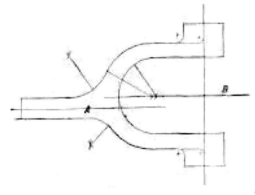

Fig. 195.

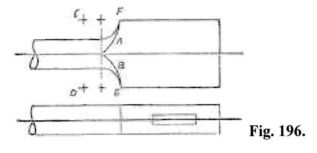

Fig. 196.

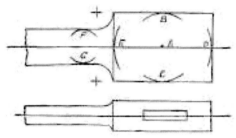

Fig. 197.

In Figure 196 is an example of a connecting rod end. From a point, as A, we draw arcs, as B C for the width, and E D for the length of the block, and through A we draw the centre line. It is obvious, however, that we may draw the centre line first, and apply the measuring rule direct to the paper, and mark lines in place of the arcs B, C, D, E, and F, G, which are for the stem. As the block joins the stem in a straight line, the latter is evidently rectangular, as will be seen by referring to Figure 197, which represents a rod end with a round stem, the fact that the stem is round being clearly shown by the curves A B. The radius of these curves is obtained as follows: It is obvious that they will join the rod stem at the same point as the shoulder curves do, as denoted by the dotted vertical line. So likewise they join the curves E F at the same point in the rod length as the shoulder curves, both curves in fact being formed by the same round corner or shoulder. The centre of the radius of A or B must therefore be the same distance from the centre of the rod as is the centre from which the shoulder curve is struck, and at the same time at such a distance from the corner (as E or F) that the curve will meet the centre line of the rod at the same point in its length as the shoulder curves do.

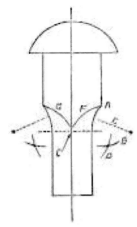

Fig. 198.

Figure 198 gives an example, in which the similar curved lines show that a part is square. The figure represents a bolt with a square under the head. As but one view is given, that fact alone tells us that it must be round or square. Now we might mark a cross on the square part, to denote that it is square; but this is unnecessary, because the curves F G show such to be the case. These curves are marked as follows: With the compasses set to the radius E, one point is rested at A, and arc B is drawn; then one point of the compass is rested at C, and arc D is drawn; giving the centre for the curve F by a similar process on the other side of the figure, curve G is drawn. Point C is obtained by drawing the dotted line across where the outline curve meets the stem. Suppose that the corner where the round stem meets the square under the head was a sharp one instead of a curve, then the traditional cross would require to be put on the square, as in Figure 199; or the cross will be necessary if the corner be a round one, if the stem is reduced in diameter, as in Figure 200.

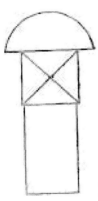

Fig. 199.

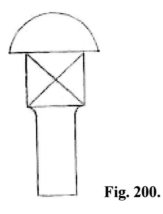

Fig. 200.

Fig. 201.

Figure 201 represents a centre punch, giving an example, in which the flat sides gradually run out upon a circle, the edges forming curves, as at A, B, etc. The length of these curves is determined as follows: They must begin where the taper of the punch joins the parallel, or at C, C, and they must end on that part of the taper stem where the diameter is equal to the diameter across the flats of the octagon. All that is to be done then is to find the diameter across the flats on the end view, and mark it on the taper stem, as at D, D, which will show where the flats terminate on the taper stem. And the curved lines, as A, B, may be drawn in by a curve that must meet at the line C, and also in a rounded point at line D.

CHAPTER VIII.

SCREW THREADS AND SPIRALS.

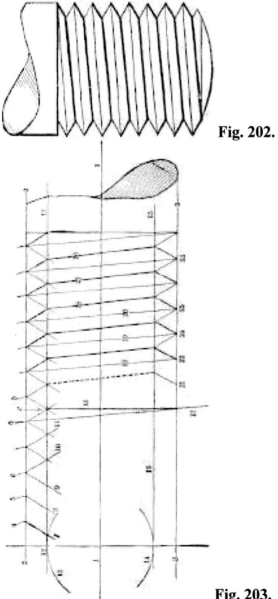

Fig. 202.

Fig. 203.

The screw thread for small bolts is represented by thick and thin lines, such as was shown in Figure 152, but in larger sizes; the angles of the thread also are drawn in, as in Figure 202, and the method of doing this is shown in Figure 203. The centre line 1 and lines 2 and 3 for the full diameter of the thread being drawn, set the compasses to the required pitch of the thread, and stepping along line 2, mark the arcs 4, 5, 6, etc., for the full length the thread is to be marked. With the triangle resting against the T-square, the lines 7, 8, 9, etc. (for the full length of the thread), are drawn from the points 4, 5, 6, on line 2. These give one side of the thread. Reversing the drawing triangle, angles 10, 11, etc., are then drawn, which will complete the outline of the thread at the top of the bolt. We may now mark the depth of the thread by drawing line 12, and with the compasses set on the centre line transfer this depth to the other side of the bolt, as denoted by the arcs 13 and 14. Touching arc 14 we mark line 15 for the thread depth on that side. We have now to get the slant of the thread across the bolt. It is obvious that in passing once around the bolt the thread advances to the amount of the pitch as from *a* to *b*; hence, in passing half way around, it will advance from *a* to *c*; we therefore draw line 16 at a right-angle to the centre line, and a line that touches the top of the threads at *a*, where it meets line 2, and also meets line 16, where it touches line 3, is the angle or slope for the tops of the threads, which may be drawn across by lines, as 18, 19, 20, etc. From these lines the sides of the thread may be drawn at the bottom of the bolt, marking first the angle on one side, as by lines 21, 22, 23, etc., and then the angles on the other, as by lines 24, 25, etc.

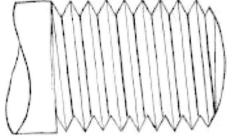

Fig. 204.

There now remain the bottoms of the thread to draw, and this is done by drawing lines from the bottom of the thread on one side of the bolt to the bottom on the other, as shown in the cut by a dotted line; hence, we may set a square blade to that angle, and mark in these lines, as 26, 27, 28, etc., and the thread is pencilled in complete.

If the student will follow out this example upon paper, it will appear to him that after the thread had been marked out on one side of the bolt, the angle of the thread might be obtained, as shown by lines 16 and 17, and that the bottoms of the thread as well as the tops might be carried across the bolt to the other side. Figure 204 represents a case in which this has been done, and it will be observed that the lines denoting the bottom of the thread do not meet the bottoms of the thread, which occurs for the reason that the angle for the bottom is not the same as that for the top of the thread.

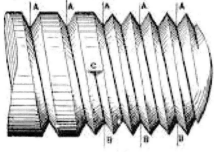

Fig. 205.

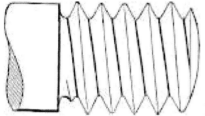

Fig. 206.

In inking in the thread, it enhances the appearance to give the bottom of the thread and the right-hand side of the same, heavy shade lines, as in Figure 202, a plan that is usually adopted for threads of large diameter and coarse pitch.

A double thread, such as in Figure 205, is drawn in the same way, except that the slant of the thread is doubled, and the square is to be set for the thread-pitch A, A, both for the tops and bottoms of the thread.

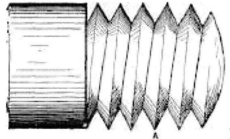

Fig 207.

A round top and bottom thread, as the Whitworth thread, is drawn by single lines, as in Figure 206. A left-hand thread, Figure 207, is obviously drawn by the same process as a right-hand one, except that the slant of the thread is given in the opposite direction.

For screw threads of a large diameter it is not uncommon to

draw in the thread curves as they appear to the eye, and the method of doing this is shown in Figure 208. The thread is first marked on both sides of the bolt, as explained, and instead of drawing, straight across the bolt, lines to represent the tops and bottoms of the thread, a template to draw the curves by is required. To get these curves, two half-circles, one equal in diameter to the top, and one equal to the bottom of the thread, are drawn, as in Figure 208.

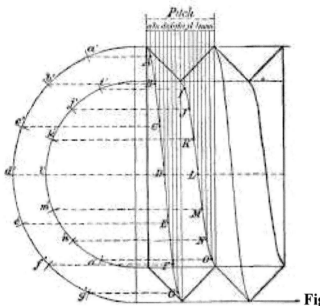

Fig. 208.

These half-circles are divided into any convenient number of equal divisions: thus in Figure 208, each has eight divisions, as *a*, *b*, *c*, etc., for the outer, and *i*, *j*, *k*, etc., for the inner one. The pitch of the thread is then divided off by vertical lines into as many equal divisions as the half-circles are divided into, as by the lines *a*, *b*, *c*, etc., to *o*. Of these, the seven from *a*, to *h*, correspond to the seven from *a'* to *g'*, and are for the top of the thread, and the seven from *i* to *o* correspond to the seven on the inner half-circle, as *i*, *j*, *k*, etc. Horizontal lines are then drawn from the points of the division to meet the vertical lines of division; thus the horizontal dotted line from *a'* meets the vertical line *a*, and where they meet, as at A, a dot is made. Where the dotted line from *b'* meets vertical line *b*, another dot is made, as at B, and so on until the point G is found. A curve drawn to pass from the top of the thread on one side of the bolt to the top of the other side, and passing through these points, as from A to G, will be the curve for the top of the thread, and from this curve a template may be made to mark all the other thread-tops from, because manifestly all the tops of the thread on the bolt will be alike.

For the bottoms of the thread, lines are similarly drawn, as from *i'* to meet *i*, where dot I is marked. J is got from *j'* and *j*, while K is got from the intersection of *k'* with *k*, and so on, the dots from I to O being those through which a curve is drawn for the bottom of the thread, and from this curve a template also may be made to mark all the thread bottoms. We have in our example used eight points of division in each half-circle, but either more or less points maybe used, the only requisite being that the pitch of the thread must be divided into as many divisions as the two half-circles are. But it is not absolutely necessary that both half-circles be divided into the same number of equal divisions. Thus, suppose the large half-circle were divided into ten divisions, then instead of the first half of the pitch being divided into eight (as from *a* to *h*) it would require to have ten lines. But the inner half-circle may have eight only, as in our example. It is more convenient, however, to use the same number of divisions for both circles, so that they may both be divided together by lines radiating from the centre. The more the points of division, the greater number of points to draw the curves through; hence it is desirable to have as many as possible, which is governed by the pitch of the thread, it being obvious that the finer the pitch the less the number of distinct and clear divisions it is practicable to divide it into. In our example the angles of the thread are spread out to cause these lines to be thrown further apart than they would be in a bolt of that diameter; hence it will be seen that in threads of but two or three inches in diameter the lines would fall very close together, and would require to be drawn finely and with care to keep them distinct.

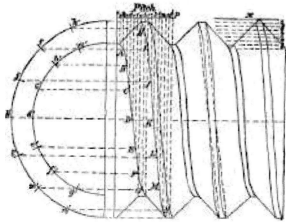

Fig. 208 a.

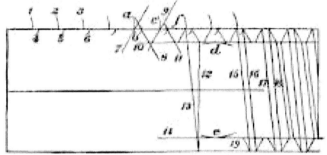

Fig. 209.

The curves for a United States standard form of thread are obtained in the same manner as from the **V** thread in Figure 208, but the thread itself is more difficult to draw. The construction of this thread is shown in Figure 208, it having a flat place at the top and at the bottom of the thread. A common **V** thread has its sides at an angle of 60 degrees, one to the other, the top and bottom meeting in a point. The United States standard is obtained from drawing a common **V** thread and dividing its depth into eight equal divisions, as at *x*, in Figure 208 *a*, and cutting off one of these divisions at the top and filling in one at the bottom to form flat places, as shown in the figure. But the thread cannot be sketched on a bolt by this means unless temporary lines are used to get the thread from, these temporary lines being drawn to represent a bolt one-fourth the depth of the thread too large in diameter. Thus, in Figure 208 *a*, it is seen that cutting off one-eighth the depth of the thread reduces the diameter of the thread. It is necessary, then, to draw the flat place on top of the thread first, the order of procedure being shown in Figure 209. The lines for the full diameter of the thread being drawn, the pitch is stepped off by arcs, as 1, 2, 3, etc.; and from these, arcs, as 4, 5, 6, etc., are marked for the width of the flat places at the tops of the threads. Then one side of the thread is marked off by lines, as 7, which meet the arcs 1, 2, 3, etc., as at *a*, *c*, etc. Similar lines, as 8 and 9, are marked for the other side of the thread, these lines, 7, 8 and 9, projecting until they cross each other. Line 10 is then drawn, making a flat place at the bottom of the thread equal in width to that at the top. Line 12 is then drawn square across the bolt, starting from the bottom of the thread, and line 13 is drawn starting from the corner *f* on one side of the thread and meeting line 12 on the other side of the thread, which gives the angle for the tops of the thread. The depth of the thread may then be marked on the other side of the bolt by the arcs *d* and *e*, and the line 14. The tops of all the threads may then be drawn in, as by lines 15, 16, 17 and 18, and by lines, as 19, etc., the thread sides may be drawn on the other side of the bolt. All that remains is to join the bottoms of the threads by lines across the bolt, and the pencil lines will be complete, ready to ink in. If the thread is to be shown curved instead of drawn straight across, the curve may be obtained by the construction in Figure 208, which is similar to that in Figure 207, except that while the pitch is divided off into 16 divisions, the whole of these 16 divisions are not used to get the curves, some of them being used twice over; thus for the bottom the eight divisions from *b* to *i* are used, while for the tops the eight from *g* to *o* are used. Hence *g*, *h* and *i* are used for getting both curves, the divisions from *a* to *b* and from *o* to *p* being taken up by the flat top and bottom of the thread. It will be noted that in Figure 207, the top of the thread is drawn first, while in Figure 208 the bottom is drawn first, and that in the latter (for the U.S. standard) the pitch is marked from centre to centre of the flats of the thread.

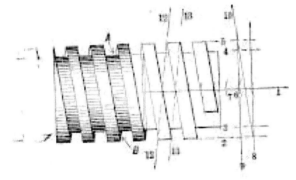

Fig. 210.

To draw a square thread the pencil lines are marked in the order shown in Figure 210, in which 1 represents the centre line and 2, 3, 4 and 5, the diameter and depth of the thread. The pitch of the thread is marked off by arcs, as 6, 7, etc., or by laying a rule directly on the centre line and marking with a lead pencil. To obtain the slant of the thread, lines 8 and 9 are drawn, and from these line 10, touching 8 and 9 where they meet lines 2 and 5; the threads may then be drawn in from the arcs as 6, 7, etc. The side of the thread will show at the top and the bottom as at A B, because of the coarse pitch and the thread on the other or unseen side of the bolt slants, as denoted by the lines 12, 13; and hence to draw the sides A B, the triangle must be set from one thread to the next on the opposite side of the bolt, as denoted by the dotted lines 12 and 13.

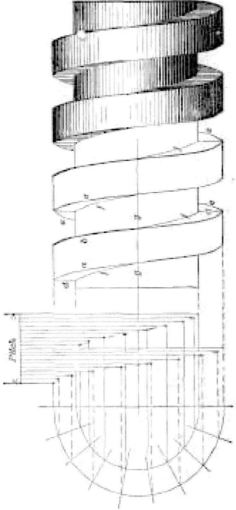

Fig. 211.

If the curves of the thread are to be drawn in, they may be obtained as in Figure 211, which is substantially the same as described for a V thread. The curves *f*, representing the sides of the thread, terminate at the centre line *g*, and the curves *e* are equidistant with the curves *c* from the vertical lines *d*. As the curves *f* above the line are the same as *f* below the line, the template for *f* need not be made to extend the whole distance across, but one-half only; as is shown by the dotted curve *g*, in the construction for finding the curve for square-threaded nuts in Figure 212.

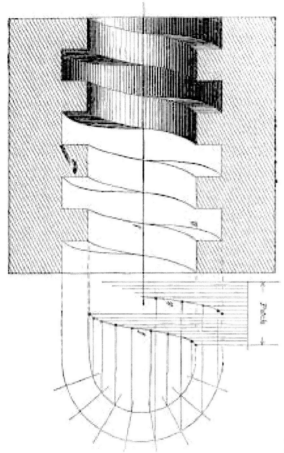

Fig. 212.

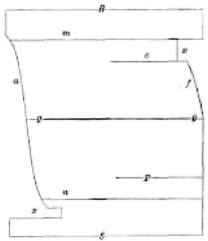

Fig. 213.

A specimen of the form of template for drawing these curves is shown in Figure 213; g g, is the centre line parallel to the edges R, S; lines m, n, represent the diameter of the thread at the top, and o, p, that at the bottom or root; edge a is formed to the points (found by the constructions in the figures as already explained) for the tops of the thread, and edge f is so formed for the curve at the thread bottoms. The edge, as S or R, is laid against the square-blade to steady it while drawing in the curves. It may be noted, however, that since the curve is the same below the centre line as it is above, the template may be made to serve for one-half the thread diameter, as at f, where it is made from o to g, only being turned upside down to draw the other half of the curve; the notches cut out at x, x, are merely to let the pencil-lines in the drawing show plainly when setting the template.

When the thread of a nut is shown in section, it slants in the opposite direction to that which appears on the bolt-thread, because it shows the thread that fits to the opposite side of the bolt, which, therefore, slants in the opposite direction, as shown by the lines 12 and 13 in Figure 210.

In a top or end view of a nut the thread depth is usually shown by a simple circle, as in Figure 214.

Fig. 214.

To draw a spiral spring, draw the centre line A, and lines B, C, Figure 215, distant apart the diameter the spring is to be less the diameter of the wire of which it is to be made. On the centre line A mark two lines a b, c d, representing the pitch of the spring. Divide the distance between a and b into four equal divisions, as by lines 1, 2, 3, letting line 3 meet line B. Line e meeting the centre line at line a, and the line B at its intersection with line 3, is the angle of the coil on one side of the spring; hence it may be marked in at all the locations, as at e f, etc. These lines give at their intersections with the lines C and B the centres for the half circles g, which being drawn, the sides h, i, j, k, etc., of the spring, may all be marked in. By the lines m, n, o, p, the other sides of the spring may be marked in.

Fig. 215.

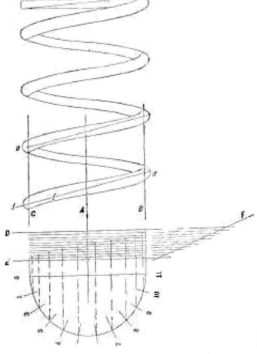

Fig. 216.

The end of the spring is usually marked straight across, as at L. If it is required to draw the coils curved instead of straight across, a template must be made, the curve being obtained as already described for threads. It may be pointed out, however, that to obtain as accurate a division as possible of the lines that divide the pitch, the pitch may be divided upon a diagonal line, as F, Figure 216, which will greatly facilitate the operation.

Before going into projections it may be as well to give some examples for practice.

CHAPTER IX.

EXAMPLES FOR PRACTICE.

Figure 217 represents a simple example for practice, which the student may draw the size of the engraving, or he may draw it twice the size. It is a locomotive spring, composed of leaves or plates, held together by a central band.

Fig. 217.

Figure 218 is an example of a stuffing box and gland, supposed to stand vertical, hence the gland has an oil cup or receptacle.

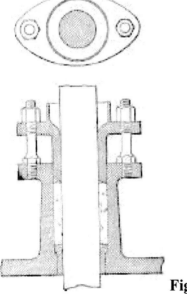

Fig. 218.

In Figure 219 are working drawings of a coupling rod, with the dimensions and directions marked in.

It may be remarked, however, that the drawings of a

workshop are, where large quantities of the same kind of work is done, varied in character to suit some special departments—that is to say, special extra drawings are made for these departments. In Figures 220 and 221 is a drawing of a connecting rod drawn, put together as it would be for the lathe, vise or erecting shop.

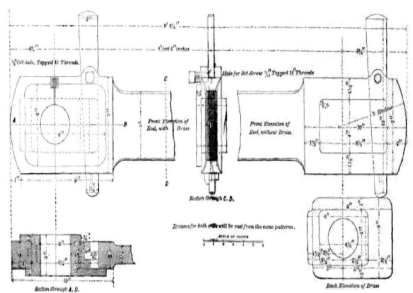

Fig. 219. (Page 169.)

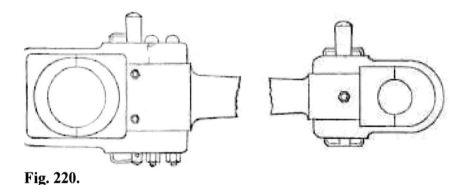

Fig. 220.

Fig. 221.

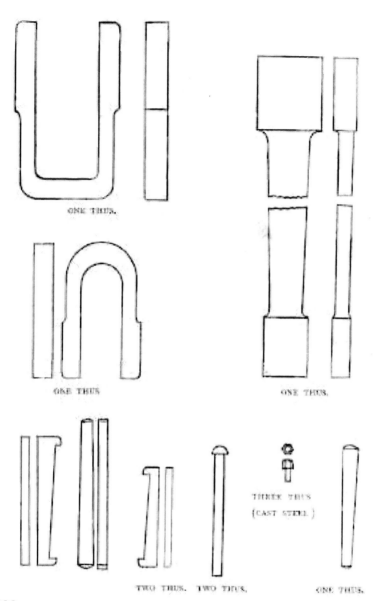

ONE THUS.

ONE THUS

ONE THUS.

THREE THUS
(CAST STEEL.)

TWO THUS.   TWO THUS.   ONE THUS.   **Fig.**

222.

To the two views shown there would be necessary detail sketches of the set screws, gibbs, and keys, all the rest being shown; the necessary dimensions being, of course, marked on the general drawing and on the details.

In so simple a thing as a connecting rod, however, there would be no question as to how the parts go together; hence detail drawings of each separate piece would answer for the lathe or vise bands.

But in many cases this would not be the case, and the

drawing would require to show the parts put together, and be accompanied with such detail sketches as might be necessary to show parts that could not be clearly defined in the general views.

The blacksmith, for example, is only concerned with the making of the separate pieces, and has no concern as to how the parts go together. Furthermore, there are parts and dimensions in the general drawing with which the blacksmith has nothing to do.

Thus the location and dimensions of the keyways, the dimensions of the brasses, and the location of the bolt holes, are matters that have no reference to the blacksmith's work, because the keyways, bolt holes, and set-screw holes would be cut out of the solid in the machine shop. It is customary, therefore, to send to the blacksmith shop drawings containing separate views of each piece drawn to the shape it is to be forged; and drawn full size, or else on a scale sufficiently large to make each part show clearly without close inspection, marking thereon the full sizes, and stating beneath the number of pieces of each detail. (As in Figure 222, which represents the iron work of the connecting rod in Figure 220). In some cases the finished sizes are marked, and it is left to the blacksmith's judgment how much to leave for the finishing. This is undesirable, because either the blacksmith is left to judge what parts are to be finished, or else there must be on the drawing instructions on this point, or else signs or symbols that are understood to convey the information. It is better, therefore, to make for the blacksmith a special sketch, and mark thereon the full-forged sizes, stating on the drawing that such is the case.

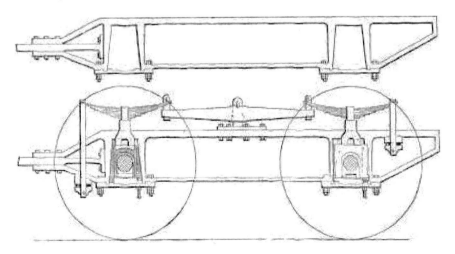

Fig. 223

As to the material of which the pieces are to be made, the

greater part of blacksmith work is made of wrought iron, and it is, therefore, unnecessary to write "wrought iron" beneath each piece. When the pieces are to be of steel, however, it should be marked on the drawing and beneath the piece. In special cases, as where the greater part of the work of the shop is of steel, the rule may, of course, be reversed, and the parts made of iron may be the ones marked, whereas when parts are sometimes of iron, and at others of steel, each piece should be marked.

As a general rule the blacksmith knows, from the custom of the shop or the nature of the work, what the quality or kind of iron is to be, and it is, therefore, only in exceptional cases that they need to be mentioned on the drawing. Thus in a carriage manufactory, Norway or Swede iron will be found, as well as the better grades of refined iron, but the blacksmith will know what iron to use, for certain parts, or the shop may be so regulated that the selection of the iron is not left to him. In marking the number of pieces required, it is better to use the word "thus" than the words "of this," or "off this," because it is shorter and more correct, for the forging is not taken off the drawing, nor is it of the same; the drawing gives the shape and the size, and the word "thus" conveys that idea better than "of," "off," or "like this."

In shops where there are many of the same pieces forged, the blacksmith is furnished with sheet-iron templates that he can lay directly upon the forging and test its dimensions at once, which is an excellent plan in large work. Such templates are, of course, made from the drawings, and it becomes a question as to whether their dimensions should be the forged or the finished ones. If they are the forged, they may cause trouble, because a forging may have a scant place that it is difficult for the blacksmith to bring up to the size of the template, and he is in doubt whether there is enough metal in the scant place to allow the job to clean up. It is better, therefore, to make them to finished sizes, so that he can see at once if the work will clean up, notwithstanding the scant place. This will lead to no errors in large work, because such work is marked out by lines, and the scant part will therefore be discovered by the machinist, who will line out the piece accordingly.

Figure 223 is a drawing of a locomotive frame, which the student may as well draw three or four times as large as the engraving, which brings us to the subject of enlarging or reducing scales.

REDUCING SCALES.

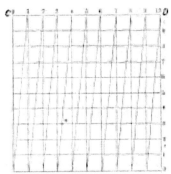

Fig. 224.

Fig. 225.

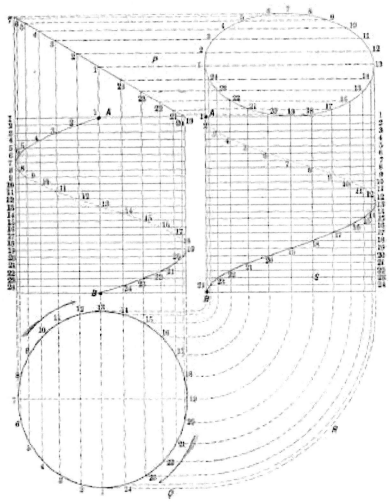

Fig. 225a.

It is sometimes necessary to reduce a drawing to a smaller scale, or to find a minute fraction of a given dimension, such fraction not being marked on the lineal measuring rules at hand. Figure 224 represents a scale for finding minute fractions. Draw seven lines parallel to each other, and equidistant draw vertical lines dividing the scale into half-inches, as at *a*, *b*, *c*, etc. Divide the first space *e d* into equal halves, draw diagonal lines, and number them as in the figure. The distance of point 1, which is at the intersection of diagonal with the second horizontal line, will be 1/24 inch from vertical line *e*. Point 2 will be 2/24 inch from line *e*, and so on. For tenths of inches there would require to be but six horizontal lines, the diagonals being drawn as before. A similar scale is shown in Figure 225. Draw the lines A B, B D, D C, C A, enclosing a square inch. Divide each of these lines into ten equal divisions, and number and letter them as shown. Draw also the diagonal lines A 1, *a* 2, B 3, and so on; then the distances from the line A C to the points of intersection of the diagonals with the horizontal lines represent hundredths of an inch.

Suppose, for example, we trace one diagonal line in its path across the figure, taking that which starts from A and ends at 1 on the top horizontal line; then where the diagonal intersects *horizontal* line 1, is 99/100 from the line B D, and 1/100 from the line A C, while where it intersects *horizontal* line 2, is 98/100 from line B D, and 2/100 from line A C, and so on. If we require to set the compasses to 67/100 inch, we set them to the radius of *n*, and the figure 3 on line B D, because from that 3 to the vertical line *d* 4 is 6/10 or 60/100 inch, and from that vertical line to the diagonal at *n* is seven divisions from the line C D of the figure.

In making a drawing to scale, however, it is an excellent plan to draw a line and divide it off to suit the required scale. Suppose, for example, that the given scale is one-quarter size, or three inches per foot; then a line three inches long may be divided into twelve equal divisions, representing twelve inches, and these may be subdivided into half or quarter inches and so on. It is recommended to the beginner, however, to spend all his time making simple drawings, without making them to scale, in order to become so familiar with the use of the instruments as to feel at home with them, avoiding the complication of early studies that would accompany drawing to scale.

CHAPTER X.

PROJECTIONS.

In projecting, the lines in one view are used to mark those in other views, and to find their shapes or curvature as they will appear in other views. Thus, in Figure 225*a* we have a spiral, wound around a cylinder whose end is cut off at an angle. The pitch of the spiral is the distance A B, and we may delineate the curve of the spiral looking at the cylinder from two positions (one at a right-angle to the other, as is shown in the figure), by means of a circle having a circumference equal to that of the cylinder.

The circumference of this circle we divide into any number of equidistant divisions, as from 1 to 24. The pitch A B of the spiral or thread is then divided off also into 24 equidistant divisions, as marked on the left hand of the figure; vertical lines are then drawn from the points of division on the circle to the points correspondingly numbered on the lines dividing the pitch; and where line 1 on the circle intersects line 1 on the pitch is one point in the curve. Similarly, where point 2 on the circle intersects line 2 on the pitch is another point in the curve, and so on for the whole 24 divisions on the circle and on the pitch. In this view, however, the path of the spiral from line 7 to line 19 lies on the other side of the cylinder, and is marked in dotted lines, because it is hidden by the cylinder. In the right-hand view, however, a different portion of the spiral or thread is hidden, namely from lines 1 to 13 inclusive, being an equal proportion to that hidden in the left-hand view.

The top of the cylinder is shown in the left-hand view to be cut off at an angle to the axis, and will therefore appear elliptical; in the right-hand view, to delineate this oval, the same vertical lines from the circle may be carried up as shown on the right hand, and horizontal lines may be drawn from the inclined face in one view across the end of the other view, as at P; the divisions on the circle may be carried up on the right-hand view by means of straight lines, as Q, and arcs of circle, as at R, and vertical lines drawn from these arcs, as line S, and where these vertical lines S intersect the horizontal lines as P, are points in the ellipse.

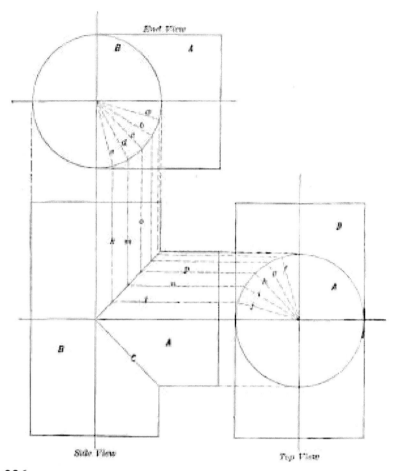

End View

Side View   *Top View*   **Fig.**

226.

Let it be required to draw a cylindrical body joining another at a right-angle; as for example, a Tee, such as in Figure 226, and the outline can all be shown in one view, but it is required to find the line of junction of one piece, A, with the other, B; that is, find or mark the lines of junction C. Now when the diameters of A and B are equal, the line of junction C is a straight line, but it becomes a curved one when the diameter of A is less than that of B, or *vice versa*; hence it may be as well to project it in both cases. For this purpose the three views are necessary. One-quarter of the circle of B, in the end view, is divided off into any number of equal divisions; thus we have chosen the divisions marked *a, b, c, d, e,* etc.; a quarter of the top view is similarly divided off, as at *f, g, h, i, j*; from these points of division lines are projected on to the side view, as shown by the dotted lines *k, l, m, n, o, p,* etc., and where these lines meet, as denoted by the dots, is in each case a point in the line of junction of the two cylinders A, B.

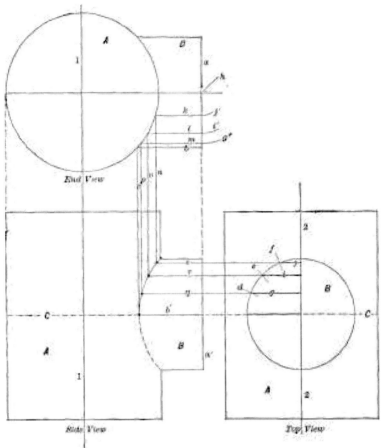

Fig.

227.

Figure 227 represents a Tee, in which B is less in diameter than A; hence the two join in a curve, which is found in a similar manner, as is shown in Figure 227. Suppose that the end and top views are drawn, and that the side view is drawn in outline, but that the curve of junction or intersection is to be found. Now it is evident that since the centre line 1 passes through the side and end views, that the face *a*, in the end view, will be even with the face *a'* in the side view, both being the same face, and as the full length of the side of B in the end view is marked by line *b*, therefore line *c* projected down from *b* will at its junction with line *b'*, which corresponds to line *b*, give the extreme depth to which *b'* extends into the body A, and therefore, the apex of the curve of intersection of B with A. To obtain other points, we divide one-quarter of the circumference of the circle B in the top view into four equal divisions, as by lines *d, e, f*, and from the points of division we draw lines *j, i, g*, to the centre line marked 2, these lines being thickened in the cut for clearness of illustration.

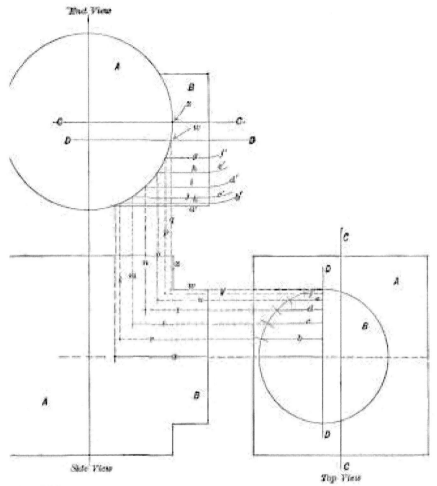

Fig. 228.

The compasses are then set to the length of thickened line *g*, and from point *h*, in the end view, as a centre, the arc *g'* is marked. With the compasses set to the length of thickened line *i*, and from *h* as a centre, arc *i'* is marked, and with the length of thickened line *j* as a radius and from *h* as a centre arc *j'* is marked; from these arcs lines *k*, *l*, *m* are drawn, and from the intersection of *k*, *l*, *m*, with the circle of A, lines *n*, *o*, *p* are let fall. From the lines of division, *d*, *e*, *f*, the lines *q*, *r*, *s* are drawn, and where lines *n*, *o*, *p* join lines *q*, *r*, *s*, are points in the curve, as shown by the dots, and by drawing a line to intersect these dots the curve is obtained on one-half of B. Since the axis of B is in the same plane as that of A, the lower half of the curve is of the same curvature as the upper, as is shown by the dotted curve.

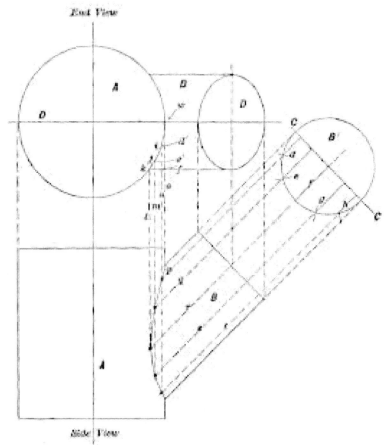

Fig. 229.

In Figure 228 the axis of piece B is not in the same plane as that of D, but to one side of it to the distance between the centre lines C, D, which is most clearly seen in the top view. In this case the process is the same except in the following points: In the side view the line *w*, corresponding to the line *w* in the end view, passes within the line *x* before the curve of intersection begins, and in transferring the lengths of the full lines *b*, *c*, *d*, *e*, *f* to the end view, and marking the arcs *b'*, *c'*, *d'*, *e'*, *f'*, they are marked from the point *w* (the point where the centre line of B intersects the outline of A), instead of from the point *x*. In all other respects the construction is the same as that in Figure 227.

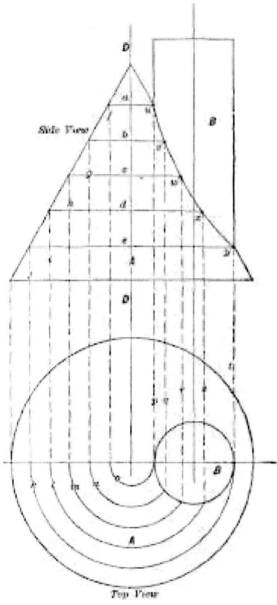

Fig. 230.

In these examples the axis of B stands at a right-angle to that of A. But in Figure 229 is shown the construction where the axis of B is not at a right-angle to A. In this case there is projected from B, in the side view, an end view of B as at B', and across this end at a right-angle to the centre line of B is marked a centre line C C of B', which is divided as before by lines *d, e, f, g, h,* their respective lengths being transferred from W as a centre, and marked by the arcs d', e', f', which are marked on a vertical line and carried by horizontal lines, to the arc of A as at i, j, k. From these points, i, j, k, the perpendicular lines l, m, n, o, are dropped, and where these lines meet lines p, q, r, s, t, are points in the curve of intersection of B with A. It will be observed that each of the lines m, n, o, serves for two of the points in the curve; thus, m meets q and s, while n meets p and t, and o meets the outline on each side of B, in the side view, and as i, j, k are obtained from d and e, the lines g and h might have been omitted, being inserted merely for the sake of illustration.

In Figure 230 is an example in which a cylinder intersects a cone, the axes being parallel. To obtain the curve of intersection in this case, the side view is divided by any convenient number of lines, as a, b, c, etc., drawn at a right-angle to its axis A A, and from one end of these lines are let fall the perpendiculars f, g, h, i, j; from the ends of these (where they meet the centre line of A in the top view), half-circles k, l, m, n, o, are drawn to meet the circle of B in the top view, and from their points of intersection with B, lines p, q, r, s, t, are drawn, and where these meet lines a, b, c, d and e, which is at u, v, w, x, y, are points in the curve.

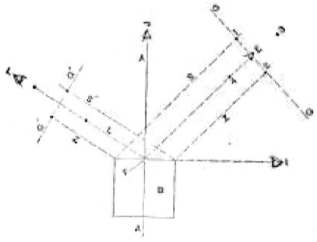

Fig. 231.

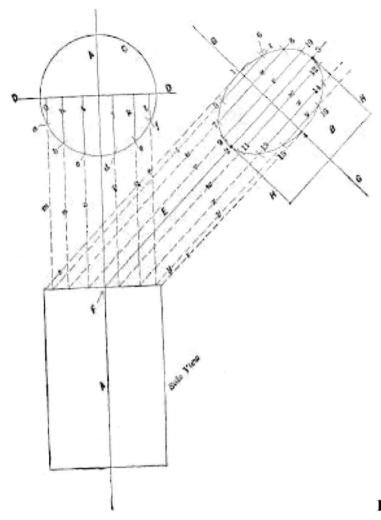

Fig. 231

a.

It will be observed, on referring again to Figure 229, that the branch or cylinder B appears to be of elliptical section on its end face, which occurs because it is seen at an angle to its end surface; now the method of finding the ellipse for any given degree of angle is as in Figure 231, in which B represents a cylindrical body whose top face would, if viewed from point I, appear as a straight line, while if viewed from point J it would appear in outline a circle. Now if viewed from point E its apparent dimension in one direction will obviously be defined by the lines S, Z. So that if on a line G G at a right angle to the line of vision E, we mark points touching lines S, Z, we get points 1 and 2, representing the apparent dimension in that direction which is the width of the ellipse. The length of the ellipse will obviously be the full diameter of the cylinder B; hence from E as a centre we mark points 3 and 4, and of the remaining points we will speak presently. Suppose now the angle the top face of B is viewed from is denoted by the line L, and lines S', Z, parallel to L, will be the width for the ellipse whose length is marked by dots, equidistant on each side of centre line G' G', which equal in their widths one from the other the full diameter of B. In this construction the ellipse will be drawn away from the cylinder B, and the ellipse, after being found, would have to be transferred to the end of B. But since centre line G G is obviously at the same angle to A A that A A is to G G, we may start from the centre line of the body whose elliptical appearance is to be drawn, and draw a centre line A A at the same angle to G G as the end of B is supposed to be viewed from. This is done in Figure 231 a, in which the end face of B is to be drawn viewed from a point on the line G G, but at an angle of 45 degrees; hence line A A is drawn at an angle of 45 degrees to centre line G G, and centre line E is drawn from the centre of the end of B at a right angle to G G, and from where it cuts A A, as at F, a side view of B is drawn, or a single line of a length equal to the diameter of B may be drawn at a right angle to A A and equidistant on each side of F. A line, D D, at a right angle to A A, and at any convenient distance above F, is then drawn, and from its intersection with A A as a centre, a circle C equal to the diameter of B is drawn; one-half of the circumference of C is divided off into any number of equal divisions as by arcs a, b, c, d, e, f. From these points of division, lines g, h, i, j, k, l are drawn, and also lines m, n, o, p, q, r. From the intersection of these last lines with the face in the side view, lines s, t, u, t, w, x, y, z are drawn, and from point F line E is drawn. Now it is clear that the width of the end face of the cylinder will appear the same from any point of view it may be looked at, hence the sides H H are made to equal the diameter of the cylinder B and marked up to centre line E.

It is obvious also that the lines s, z, drawn from the extremes of the face to be projected will define the width of the ellipse, hence we have four of the points (marked respectively 1, 2, 3, 4) in the ellipse. To obtain the remaining points, lines t, u, v, w, x, y (which start from the point on the face F where the lines m, n, o, p, q, r, respectively meet it) are drawn across the face of B as shown. The compasses are then set to the radius g; that is, from centre line D to division a on the circle, and this radius is transferred to the face to be projected the compass-point being rested at the intersection of centre line G and line t, and two arcs as 5 and 6 drawn, giving two more points in the curve of the ellipse.

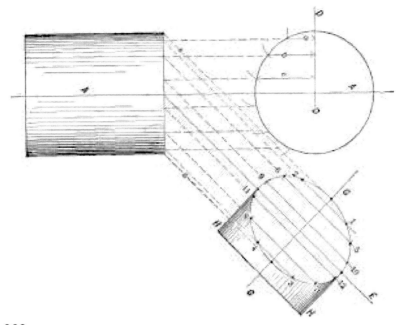

Fig. 232.

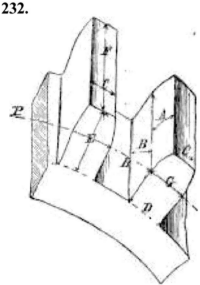

Fig. 233.

The compasses are then set to the length of line *h* (that is, from centre line D to point of division *b*), and this distance is transferred, setting the compasses on centre line G where it is intersected by line *u*, and arcs 7, 8 are marked, giving two more points in the ellipse. In like manner points 9 and 10 are obtained from the length of line *i*, 11 and 12 from that of *j*; points 13 and 14 from the length of *k*, and 15 and 16 from *l*, and the ellipse may be drawn in from these points.

It may be pointed out, however, that since points 5 and 6 are the same distance from G that points 15 and 16 are, and since points 7 and 8 are the same distance from G that points 13 and 14 are, while points 9 and 10 are the same distance from G that 11 and 12 are, the lines, *j*, *k*, *l* are unnecessary, since *l* and *g* are of equal length, as are also *h* and *k* and *i* and *j*. In Figure 232 the cylinders are line shaded to make them show plainer to the eye, and but three lines (*a*, *b*, *c*) are used to get the radius wherefrom to mark the arcs where the points in the ellipse shall fall; thus, radius *a* gives points 1, 2, 3 and 4; radius *b* gives points 5, 6, 7 and 8, and radius *c* gives 9, 10, 11 and 12, the extreme diameter being obtained from lines S, Z, and H, H.

CHAPTER XI.

DRAWING GEAR WHEELS.

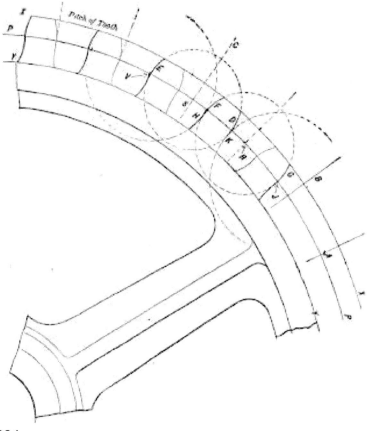

Fig. 234.

The names given to the various lines of a tooth on a gear-wheel are as follows:

In Figure 233, A is the face and B the flank of a tooth, while C is the point, and D the root of the tooth; E is the height or depth, and F the breadth. P P is the pitch circle, and the space between the two teeth, as H, is termed a space.

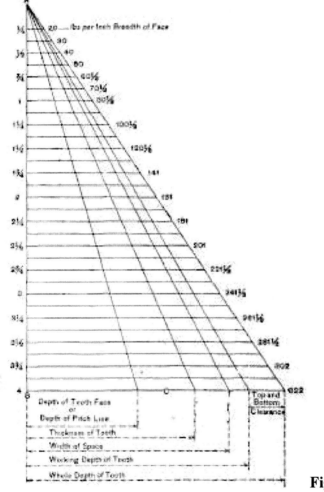

Fig. 235.

It is obvious that the points of the teeth and the bottoms of the spaces, as well as the pitch circle, are concentric to the axis of the wheel bore. And to pencil in the teeth these circles must be fully drawn, as in Figure 234, in which P P is the pitch circle. This circle is divided into as many equal divisions as the wheel is to have teeth, these divisions being denoted by the radial lines, A, B, C, etc.

Where these divisions intersect the pitch circle are the centres from which all the teeth curves may be drawn. The compasses are set to a radius equal to the pitch, less one-half the thickness of the tooth, and from a centre, as R, two face curves, as F G, may be marked; from the next centre, as at S, the curves D E may be marked, and so on for all the faces; that is, the tooth curves lying between the outer circle X and the pitch circle P. For the flank curves, that is, the curve from P to Y, the compasses are set to a radius equal to the pitch; and from the sides of the teeth the flank curves are drawn. Thus from J, as a centre flank, K is drawn; from V, as a centre flank, H is drawn, and so on.

The proportions of the teeth for cast gears generally accepted in this country are those given by Professor Willis, as average practice, and are as follows:

Depth to pitch line, 3/10 of the pitch. Working depth, 6/10 " " Whole depth, 7/10 " " Thickness of tooth, 5/11 " " Breadth of space, 6/11 " "

Instead, however, of calculating the dimensions these proportions give for any particular pitch, a diagram or scale may be made from which they may be taken for any pitch by a direct application of the compasses. A scale of this kind is given in Figure 235, in which the line A B is divided into inches and parts to represent the pitches; its total length representing the coarsest pitch within the capacity of the scale; and, the line B C (at a right-angle to A B) the whole depth of the tooth for the coarsest pitch, being 7/10 of the length of A B.

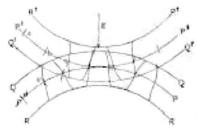

Fig. 236.

The other diagonal lines are for the proportion of the dimensions marked on the figure. Thus the depth of face, or distance from the pitch line to the extremity or tooth point for a 4 inch pitch, would be measured along the line B C, from the vertical line B to the first diagonal. The thickness of the tooth would be for a 4 inch pitch along line B C from B to the second diagonal, and so on. For a 3 inch pitch the measurement would be taken along the horizontal line, starting from the 3 on the line A B, and so on. On the left of the diagram or scale is marked the lbs. strain each pitch will safely transmit per inch width of wheel face, according to Professor Marks.

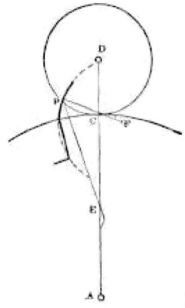

Fig. 237.

The application of the scale as follows: The pitch circles P P and P' P', Figure 236, for the respective wheels, are drawn, and the height of the teeth is obtained from the scale and marked beyond the pitch circles, when circles Q and Q' may be drawn. Similarly, the depths of the teeth within the pitch circles are obtained from the scale or diagram and marked within the respective pitch circles, and circles R and R' are marked in. The pitch circles are divided off into as many points of equal division, as at *a, b, c, d, e*, etc., as the respective wheels are to have teeth, and the thickness of tooth having been obtained from the scale, this thickness is marked from the points of division on the pitch circles, as at *f* in the figure, and the tooth curves may then be drawn in. It may be observed, however, that the tooth thicknesses will not be strictly correct, because the scale gives the same chord pitch for the teeth on both wheels which will give different arc pitches to the teeth on the two wheels; whereas, it is the arc pitches, and not the chord pitches, that should be correct. This error obviously increases as there is a greater amount of difference between the two wheels.

The curves given to the teeth in Figure 234 are not the proper ones to transmit uniform motion, but are curves merely used by draughtsmen to save the trouble of finding the true curves, which if it be required, may be drawn with a very near approach to accuracy, as follows, which is a construction given by Rankine:

Draw the rolling circle D, Figure 237, and draw A D, the line of centres. From the point of contact at C, mark on D, a point distant from C one-half the amount of the pitch, as at P, and draw the line P C of indefinite length beyond C. Draw the line P E passing through the line of centres at E, which is equidistant between C and A. Then increase the length of line P F to the right of C by an amount equal to the radius A C, and then diminish it to an amount equal to the radius E D, thus obtaining the point F and the latter will be the location of centre for compasses to strike the face curve.

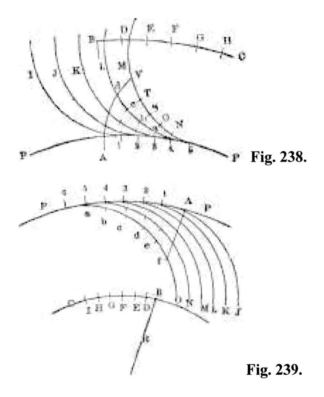

Fig. 238.

Fig. 239.

Another method of finding the face curve, with compasses, is as follows: In Figure 238 let P P represent the pitch circle of the wheel to be marked, and B C the path of the centre of the generating or describing circle as it rolls outside of P P. Let the point B represent the centre of the generating circle when it is in contact with the pitch circle at A. Then from B mark off, on B C, any number of equidistant points, as D, E, F, G, H, and from A mark on the pitch circle, with the same radius, an equal number of points of division, as 1, 2, 3, 4, 5. With the compasses set to the radius of the generating circle, that is, A B, from B, as a centre, mark the arc I, from D, the arc J, from E, the arc K, from F, and so on, marking as many arcs as there are points of division on B C. With the compasses set to the radius of divisions 1, 2, etc., step off on arc M the five divisions, N, O, S, T, V, and at V will be a point on the epicycloidal curve. From point of division 4, step off on L four points of division, as *a*, *b*, *c*, *d*; and *d* will be another point on the epicycloidal curve. From point 3, set off three divisions, and so on, and through the points so obtained draw by hand, or with a scroll, the curve.

Hypocycloids for the flanks of the teeth maybe traced in a similar manner. Thus in Figure 239, P P is the pitch circle, and B C the line of motion of the centre of the generating circle to be rolled within P P. From 1 to 6 are points of equal division on the pitch circle, and D to I are arc locations for the centre of the generating circle. Starting from A, which represents the location for the centre of the generating circle, the point of contact between the generating and base circles will be at B. Then from 1 to 6 are points of equal division on the pitch circle, and from D to I are the corresponding locations for the centres of the generating circle. From these centres the arcs J, K, L, M, N, O, are struck. The six divisions on O, from *a* to *f*, give at *f* a point in the curve. Five divisions on N, four on M, and so on, give, respectively, points in the curve.

There is this, however, to be noted concerning the construction of the last two figures. Since the circle described by the centre of the generating circle is of a different arc or curve to that of the pitch circle, the length of an arc having an equal radius on each will be different. The amount is so small as to be practically correct. The direction of the error is to give to the curves a less curvature, as though they had been produced by a generating circle of larger diameter. Suppose, for example, that the difference between the arc *a*, *b*, and its chord is .1, and that the difference between the arc 4, 5, and its chord is .01, then the error in one step is .09, and, as the point *f* is formed in five steps, it will contain this error multiplied five times. Point *d* would contain it multiplied three times, because it has three steps, and so on.

The error will increase in proportion as the diameter of the generating is less than that of the pitch circle, and though in large wheels, working with large wheels, so that the difference between the radius of the generating circle and that of the smallest wheel is not excessive, it is so small as to be practically inappreciable, yet in small wheels, working with large ones, it may form a sensible error.

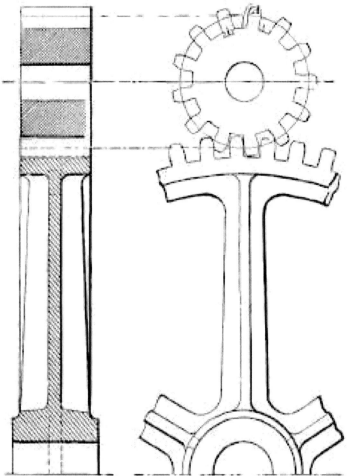

Fig. 240.

For showing the dimensions through the arms and hub, a sectional view of a section of the wheel may be given, as in Figure 240, which represents a section of a wheel, and a pinion, and on these two views all the necessary dimensions may be marked.

If it is desired to draw an edge view of a wheel (which the student will find excellent practice), the lines for the teeth may be projected from the teeth in the side view, as in Figure 240 *a*. Thus tooth E is projected by drawing lines from the corners A, B, C, in the side view across the face in the edge view, as at A, B, C in the latter view, and similar lines may be obtained in the same way for all the teeth.

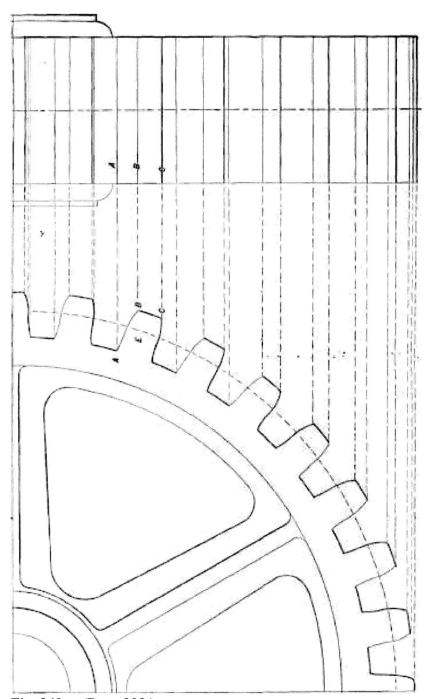

Fig. 240 a. (Page 203.)

When the teeth of wheels are to be cut to form in a
gear-cutting machine, the thickness of the teeth is nearly equal to the

thickness of the spaces, there being just sufficient difference to prevent the teeth of one wheel from becoming locked in the spaces of the other; but when the teeth are to be cast upon the wheel, the tooth thickness is made less than the width of the space to an amount that is usually a certain proportion of the pitch, and is termed the side clearance. In all wheels, whether with cut or cast teeth, there is given a certain amount of top and bottom clearance; that is to say, the points of the teeth of one wheel do not reach to the bottom of the spaces in the other. Thus in the Pratt and Whitney system the top and bottom clearance is one-eighth of the pitch, while in the Brown and Sharpe system for involute teeth the clearance is equal to one-tenth the thickness of the tooth.

In drawing bevil gear wheels, the pitch line of each tooth on each wheel, and the surfaces of the points, as well as those at the bottom of the spaces, must all point to a centre, as E in Figure 241, which centre is where the axes of the shafts would meet. It is unnecessary to mark in the correct curves for the teeth, for reasons already stated, with reference to the curves for a spur wheel. But if it is required to do so, the construction to find the curves is as shown in Figure 242, in which let A A represent the axis of one shaft, and B that of the other of the pair of bevil wheels that are to work together, their axes meeting at W; draw the line E at a right angle to A A, and representing the pitch circle diameter of one wheel, and draw F at a right angle to B, and representing the pitch circle of the other wheel; draw the line G G, passing through the point W and the point T, where the pitch circles or lines E F meet, and G G will be the line of contact of the tooth of one wheel upon the tooth of the other wheel; or in other words, the pitch line of the tooth.

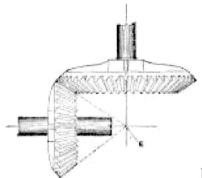

Fig. 241.

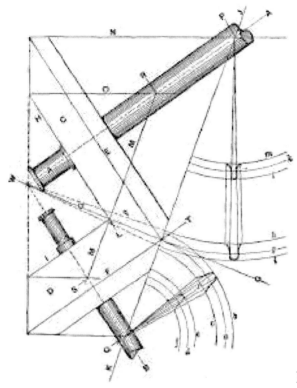

Fig. 242.

Draw lines, as H and I, representing the tooth breadth. From W, as a centre, draw on each side of G G dotted lines, as P, representing the height of the tooth above and below the pitch line G G. At a right angle to G G draw the line J K; and from where this line meets B, as at Q, mark the arc *a*, which will represent the pitch circle for the large diameter of the pinion D. [The smallest wheel of a pair of gears is termed the pinion.] Draw the arc *b* for the height, and circle *c* for the depth of the teeth, thus defining the height of the tooth at that end. Similarly from P, as a centre mark (for the large diameter of wheel C,) arcs *g*, *h*, and *i*, arc *g* representing the pitch circle, *i* the height, and *h* the depth of the tooth. On these arcs draw the proper tooth curves in the same manner as for spur wheels; that is, obtain the curves by the construction shown in Figures 237, or by those in Figures 238 and 239.

To obtain the arcs for the other end of the tooth, draw line M M parallel to line J K; set the compasses to the radius R L, and from P, as a centre, draw the pitch circle *k*. For the depth of the tooth draw the dotted line *p*, meeting the circle *h* and the point W. A similar line, from *i* to W, will give the height of the tooth at its inner end. Then the tooth curves may be drawn on these three arcs, *k*, *l*, *m*, in the same as if they were for a spur wheel.

Similarly for the pitch circle of the inner and small end of the pinion teeth, set the compasses to radius S L, and from Q as a centre mark the pitch circle *d*. Outside of *d* mark *e* for the height above pitch lines of the tooth, and inside of *d* mark the arc *f* for the depth below pitch line of the tooth at that end. The distance between the dotted lines as *p*, represents the full height of the tooth; hence *h* meets *p*, which is the root of the tooth on the large wheel. To give clearance and prevent the tops of the teeth on one wheel from bearing against the bottoms of the spaces in the other wheel, the point of the pinion teeth is marked below; thus arc *b* does not meet *h* or *p*, but is short to the amount of clearance. Having obtained the arcs *d*, *e*, *f*, the curves may be marked thereon as for a spur wheel. A tooth thus marked is shown at *x*, and from its curves between *b* and *c*, a template may be made for the large diameter or outer end of the pinion teeth. Similarly for the wheel C the outer end curves are marked on the arcs *g*, *h*, *i*, and those for the other end of the tooth are marked between the arcs *l*, *m*.

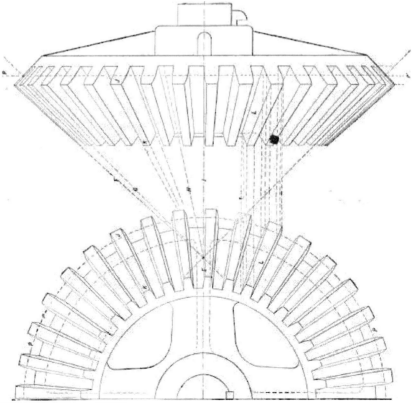

Fig. 243. (Page 207.)

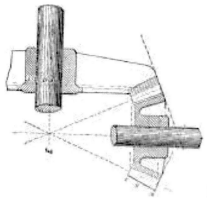

Fig. 244.

Figure 243 represents a drawing of one-half of a bevil gear, and an edge view projected from the same. The point E corresponds to point E in Figure 241, or W in 242. The line F shows that the top surface of the teeth points to E. Line G shows that the pitch line of each tooth points to E, and lines H show that the bottom of the surface of a space also points to E. Line 1 shows that the sides of each tooth point to E. And it follows that the outer end of a tooth is both higher or deeper and also thicker than its inner end; thus J is thicker and deeper than end K of the tooth. Lines F G, representing the top and bottom of a tooth in Figure 243, obviously correspond to dotted lines *p* in Figure 242. The outer and inner ends of the teeth in the edge view are projected from the outer and inner ends in the face view, as is shown by the dotted lines carried from tooth L in the face view, to tooth L in the edge view, and it is obvious from what has been said that in drawing the lines for the tooth in the edge view they will point to the centre E.

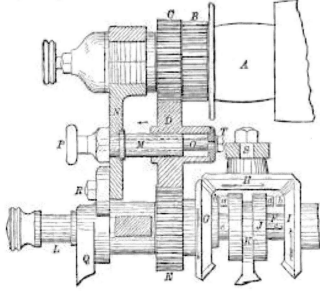

Fig. 245.

To save work in drawing bevil gear wheels, they are sometimes drawn in section or in outline only; thus in Figure 244 is shown a pair of bevil wheels shown in section, and in Figure 245 is a drawing of a part of an Ames lathe feed motion. B C D and E are spur gears, while G H and I are bevil gears, the cone surface on which the teeth lie being left blank, save at the edges where a tooth is in each case drawn in. Wheel D is shown in section so as to show the means by which it may be moved out of gear with C and E. Small bevil gears may also be represented by simple line shading; thus in Figure 247 the two bodies A and C would readily be understood to be a bevil gear and pinion. Similarly small spur wheels

may be represented by simple circles in a side view and by line shading in an edge view; thus it would answer every practical purpose if such small wheels as in Figures 246 and 247 at D, F, G, K, P, H, I and J, were drawn as shown. The pitch circles, however, are usually drawn in red ink to distinguish them.

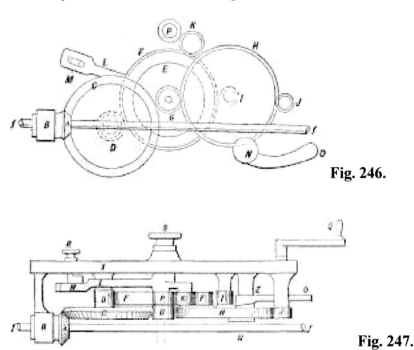

Fig. 246.

Fig. 247.

In Figure 248 is an example in which part of the gear is shown with teeth in, and the remainder is illustrated by circles.

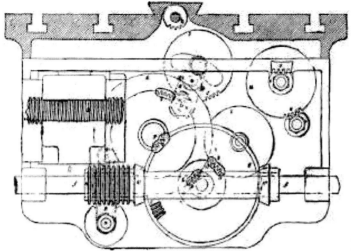

Fig. 248.

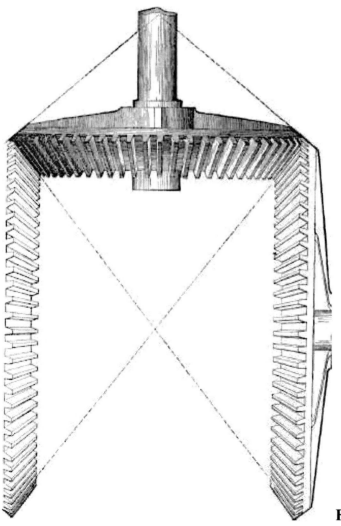

Fig. 249.

In Figure 250 is a drawing of part of the feed motions of a Niles Tool Works horizontal boring mill, Figure 251 being an end view of the same, *f* is a friction disk, and *g* a friction pinion, *g'* is a rack, F is a feed-screw, *p* is a bevil pinion, and *q* a bevil wheel; *i, m, o,* are gear wheels, and *J* a worm operating a worm-pinion and the gears shown.

Figure 249 represents three bevil gears, the upper of which is line shaded, forming an excellent example for the student to copy.

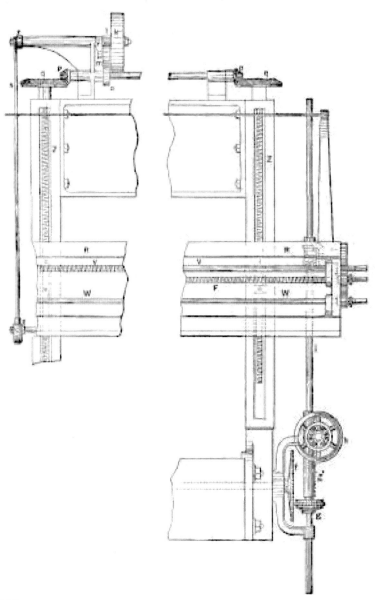

Fig.

250.

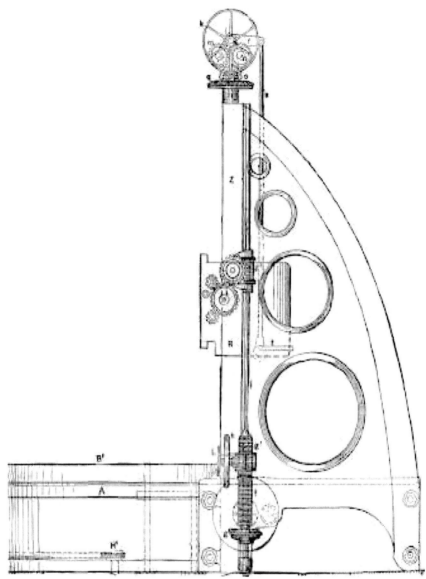

Fig. 251. (Page 209.)

The construction of oval gearing is shown in Figures 252, 253, 254, 255, and 256. The pitch-circle is drawn by the construction for drawing an ellipse that was given with reference to Figure 81, but as that construction is by means of arcs of circles, and therefore not strictly correct, Professor McCord, in an article on elliptical gearing, says, concerning it and the construction of oval gearing generally, as follows:

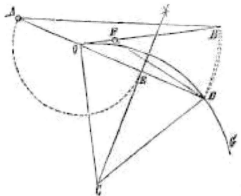

Fig. 252.

But these circular arcs may be rectified and subdivided with great facility and accuracy by a very simple process, which we take from Prof. Rankine's "Machinery and Mill Work," and is illustrated in Figure 252. Let O B be tangent at O to the arc O D, of which C is the centre. Draw the chord D O, bisect it in E, and produce it to A, making O A=O E; with centre A and radius A D describe an arc cutting the tangent in B; then O B will be very nearly equal in length to the arc O D, which, however, should not exceed about 60 degrees; if it be 60 degrees, the error is theoretically about 1/900 of the length of the arc, O B being so much too short; but this error varies with the fourth power of the angle subtended by the arc, so that for 30 degrees it is reduced to 1/16 of that amount, that is, to 1/14400. Conversely, let O B be a tangent of given length; make O F=1/4 O B; then with centre F and radius F B describe an arc cutting the circle O D G (tangent to O B at O) in the point D; then O D will be approximately equal to O B, the error being the same as in the other construction and following the same law.

The extreme simplicity of these two constructions and the facility with which they may be made with ordinary drawing instruments make them exceedingly convenient, and they should be more widely known than they are. Their application to the present problem is shown in Figure 253, which represents a quadrant of an ellipse, the approximate arcs C D, E, E F, F A having been determined by trial and error. In order to space this off, for the positions of the teeth, a tangent is drawn at D, upon which is constructed the rectification of D C, which is D G, and also that of D E in the opposite direction, that is, D H, by the process just explained. Then, drawing the tangent at F, we set off in the same manner F I = F E, and F K = F A, and then measuring H L = I K, we have finally G L, equal to the whole quadrant of the ellipse.

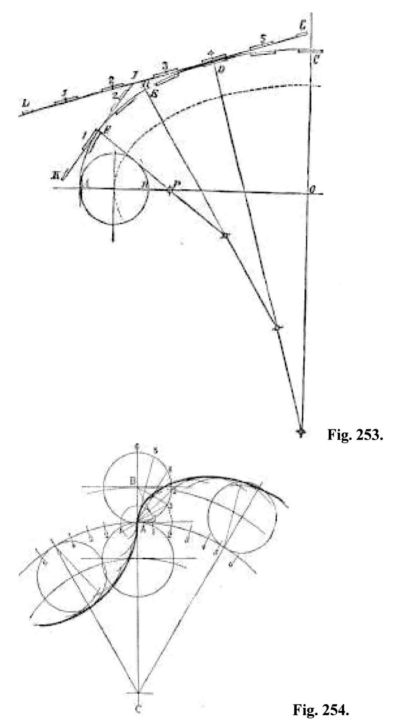

Fig. 253.

Fig. 254.

Let it now be required to lay out twenty-four teeth upon this ellipse; that is, six in each quadrant; and for symmetry's sake we will suppose that the centre of one tooth is to be at A, and that of another at C, Figure 253. We, therefore, divide L G into six equal parts at the points 1, 2, 3, etc., which will be the centres of the teeth upon the rectified ellipse. It is practically necessary to make the spaces a little greater than the teeth; but if the greatest attainable exactness in the operation of the wheels is aimed at, it is important to observe that backlash, in elliptical gearing, has an effect quite different from that resulting in the case of circular wheels. When the pitch-curves are circles, they are always in contact; and we may, if we choose, make the tooth only half the breadth of the space, so long as its outline is correct. When the motion of the driver is reversed, the follower will stand still until the backlash is taken up, when the motion will go on with a perfectly constant velocity ratio as before. But in the case of two elliptical wheels, if the follower stand still while the driver moves, which must happen when the motion is reversed if backlash exists, the pitch-curves are thrown out of contact, and, although the continuity of the motion will not be interrupted, the velocity ratio will be affected. If the motion is never to be reversed, the perfect law of the velocity ratio due to the elliptical pitch-curve may be preserved by reducing the thickness of the tooth, not equally on each side, as is done in circular wheels, but wholly on the side not in action. But if the machine must be capable of acting indifferently in both directions, the reduction must be made on both sides of the tooth: evidently the action will be slightly impaired, for which reason the backlash should be reduced to a minimum. Precisely what *is* the minimum is not so easy to say, as it evidently depends much upon the excellence of the tools and the skill of the workman. In many treatises on constructive mechanism it is variously stated that the backlash should be from one-fifteenth to one-eleventh of the pitch, which would seem to be an ample allowance in reasonably good castings not intended to be finished, and quite excessive if the teeth are to be cut; nor is it very obvious that its amount should depend upon the pitch any more than upon the precession of the equinoxes. On paper, at any rate, we may reduce it to zero, and make the teeth and spaces equal in breadth, as shown in the figure, the teeth being indicated by the double lines. Those upon the portion L H are then laid off upon K I, after which these divisions are transferred to the ellipse by the second of Prof. Rankine's constructions, and we are then ready to draw the teeth.

The outlines of these, as of any other teeth upon pitch-curves which roll together in the same plane, depend upon the general law that they must be such as can be marked out upon the planes of the curves, as they roll by a tracing-point, which is rigidly connected with and carried by a third line, moving in rolling contact with both the pitch-curves. And since under that condition the motion of this third line, relatively to each of the others, is the same as though it rolled along each of them separately while they remained fixed, the process of constructing the generated curves becomes comparatively simple. For the describing line we naturally select a circle, which, in order to fulfil the condition, must be small enough to roll within the pitch ellipse; its diameter is determined by the consideration that if it be equal to A P, the radius of the arc A F, the flanks of the teeth in that region will be radial. We have, therefore, chosen a circle whose diameter, A B, is three-fourths of A P, as shown, so that the teeth, even at the ends of the wheels, will be broader at the base than on the pitch line. This circle ought strictly to roll upon the true elliptical curve; and assuming, as usual, the tracing-point upon the circumference, the generated curves would vary slightly from true epicycloids, and no two of those used in the same quadrant of the ellipse would be exactly alike. Were it possible to divide the ellipse accurately, there would be no difficulty in laying out these curves; but having substituted the circular arcs, we must now roll the generating circle upon these as bases, thus forming true epicycloidal teeth, of which those lying upon the same approximating arc will be exactly alike. Should the junction of two of these arcs fall within the breadth of a tooth, as at D, evidently both the face and the flank on one side of that tooth will be different from those on the other side; should the junction coincide with the edge of a tooth, which is very nearly the case at F, then the face on that side will be the epicycloid belonging to one of the arcs, its flank a hypocycloid belonging to the other; and it is possible that either the face or the flank on one side should be generated by the rolling of the describing circle partly on one arc, partly on the one adjacent, which, upon a large scale, and where the best results are aimed at, may make a sensible change in the form of the curve.

The convenience of the constructions given in Figure 252 is nowhere more apparent than in the drawing of the epicycloids, when, as in the case in hand the base and generating circles may be of incommensurable diameters; for which reason we have, in Figure 254, shown its application in connection with the most rapid and accurate mode yet known of describing those curves. Let C be the centre of the base circle; B, that of the rolling one; A, the point of contact. Divide the semi-circumference of B into six equal parts at 1, 2, 3, etc.; draw the common tangent at A, upon which rectify the arc A 2 by process No. 1; then by process No. 2 set out an equal arc A 2 on the base circle, and stepping it off three times to the right and left, bisect these spaces, thus making subdivisions on the base circle equal in length to those on the rolling one. Take in succession as radii the chords A 1, A 2, A 3, etc., of the describing circle, and with centres 1, 2, 3, etc., on the base circle, strike arcs either externally or internally, as shown respectively on the right and left; the curve tangent to the external arcs is the epicycloid, that tangent to the internal ones the hypocycloid, forming the face and flank of a tooth for the base circle.

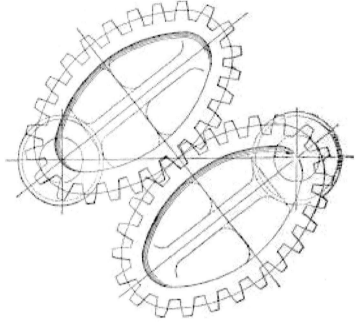

Fig. 255.

In the diagram, Figure 253, we have shown a part of an ellipse whose length is ten inches, and breadth six, the figure being half size. In order to give an idea of the actual appearance of the combination when complete, we show in Figure 255 the pair in gear, on a scale of three inches to the foot. The excessive eccentricity was selected merely for the purpose of illustration. Figure 255 will serve also to call attention to another serious circumstance, which is, that although the ellipses are alike, the wheels are not; nor can they be made so if there be an even number of teeth, for the obvious reason that a tooth upon one wheel must fit into a space on the other; and since in the first wheel, Figure 255, we chose to place a tooth at the extremity of each axis, we must in the second one place there a space instead; because at one time the major axes must coincide; at another, the minor axes, as in Figure 255. If, then, we use even numbers, the distribution, and even the forms of the teeth, are not the same in the two wheels of the pair. But this complication may be avoided by using an odd number of teeth, since, placing a tooth at one extremity of the major axes, a space will come at the other.

It is not, however, always necessary to cut teeth all round these wheels, as will be seen by an examination of Figure 256, C and D being the fixed centres of the two ellipses in contact at P. Now P must be on the line C D, whence, considering the free foci, we see that P B is equal to P C, and P A to P D; and the common tangent at P makes equal angles with C P and P A, as is also with P B and P D; therefore, C D being a straight line, A B is also a straight line and equal to C D. If then the wheels be overhung, that is, fixed on the ends of the shafts outside the bearings, leaving the outer faces free, the moving foci may be connected by a rigid link A B, as shown.

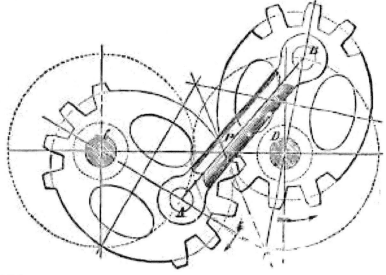

Fig. 256.

This link will then communicate the same motion that would result from the use of the complete elliptical wheels, and we may therefore dispense with the most of the teeth, retaining only those near the extremities of the major axes, which are necessary in order to assist and control the motion of the link at and near the dead-points. The arc of the pitch-curves through which the teeth must extend will vary with their eccentricity; but in many cases it would not be greater than that which in the approximation may be struck about one centre; so that, in fact, it would not be necessary to go through the process of rectifying and subdividing the quarter of the ellipse at all, as in this case it can make no possible difference whether the spacing adopted for the teeth to be cut would "come out even" or not, if carried around the curve. By this expedient, then, we may save not only the trouble of drawing, but a great deal of labor in making, the teeth round the whole ellipse. We might even omit the intermediate portions of the pitch ellipses themselves; but as they move in rolling contact their retention can do no harm, and in one part of the movement will be beneficial, as they will do part of the work; for if, when turning, as shown by the arrows, we consider the wheel whose axis is D as the driver, it will be noted that its radius of contact, C P, is on the increase; and so long as this is the case the other wheel will be compelled to move by contact of the pitch lines, although the link be omitted. And even if teeth be cut all round the wheels, this link is a comparatively inexpensive and a useful addition to the combination, especially if the eccentricity be considerable. Of course the wheels shown in Figure 255 might also have been made alike, by placing a tooth at one end of the major axis and a space at the other, as above suggested. In regard to the variation in the velocity ratio, it will be seen, by reference to Figure 256, that if D be the axis of the driver, the follower will in the position there shown move faster, the ratio of the angular velocities being $P \times D/P \times B$; if the driver turn uniformly, the velocity of the follower will diminish, until at the end of half a revolution, the velocity ratio will be $P \times B/P \times D$; in the other half of the revolution these changes will occur in a reverse order. But $P\ D = L\ B$; if then the centres B D are given in position, we know L P, the major axis; and in order to produce any assumed maximum or minimum velocity ratio, we have only to divide L P into segments whose ratio is equal to that assumed value, which will give the foci of the ellipse, whence the minor axis may be found and the curve described. For instance, in Figure 255 the velocity ratio being nine to one at the maximum, the major axis is divided into two parts, of which one is nine times as long as the other; in Figure 256 the ratio is as one to three, so that the major axis being divided into four parts, the distance A C between the foci is equal to two of them, and the distance of either focus from the nearest extremity of the major axis is equal to one, and from the more remote extremity is equal to three of these parts.

CHAPTER XII.

PLOTTING MECHANICAL MOTIONS.

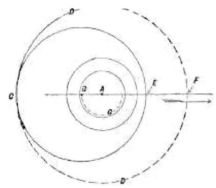

Fig. 257.

Let it be required to find how much motion an eccentric will give to its rod, the distance from the centre of its bore to the centre of the circumference, which is called the throw, being the distance from A to B in Figure 257. Now as the eccentric is moved around by the shaft, it is evident that the axis of its motion will be the axis A of the shaft. Then from A as a centre, and with radius from A to C, we draw the dotted circle D, and from E to F will be the amount of motion of the rod in the direction of the arrow.

This becomes obvious if we suppose a lead pencil to be placed against the eccentric at E, and suppose the eccentric to make half a revolution, whereupon the pencil will be pushed out to F. If now we measure the distance from E to F, we shall find it is just twice that from A to B. We may find the amount of motion, however, in another way, as by striking the dotted half circle G, showing the path of motion of B, the diameter of this path of motion being the amount of lateral motion given to the rod.

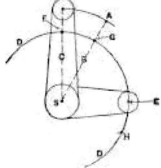

Fig. 258.

In Figure 258 is a two arm lever fast upon the same axis or shaft, and it is required to find how much a given amount of motion of the long arm will move the short one. Suppose the distance the long arm moves is to A. Then draw the line B from A to the axis of the shaft, and the line C the centre line of the long arm. From the axis of the shaft as a centre, draw the circle D, passing through the eye or centre E of the short arm. Take the radius from F to G, and from E as a centre mark it on D as at H, and H is where E will be when the long arm moves to A. We have here simply decreased the motion in the same proportion as one arm is shorter than the other. The principle involved is to take the motion of both arms at an equal distance from their axis of motion, which is the axis of the shaft S.

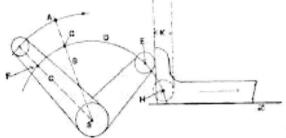

Fig. 259.

In Figure 259 we have a case in which the end of a lever acts directly upon a shoe. Now let it be required to find how much a given motion of the lever will cause the shoe to slide along the line x; the point H is here found precisely as before, and from it as a centre, the dotted circle equal in diameter to the small circle at E is drawn from the perimeter of the dotted circle, a dotted line is carried up and another is carried up from the face of the shoe. The distance K between these dotted lines is the amount of motion of the shoe.

In Figure 260 we have the same conditions as in Figure 259, but the short arm has a roller acting against a larger roller R. The point H is found as before. The amount of motion of R is the distance of K from J; hence we may transfer this distance from the centre of R, producing the point P, from which the new position may be marked by a dotted circle as shown.

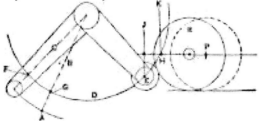

Fig. 260.

In Figure 261 a link is introduced in place of the roller, and it is required to find the amount of motion of rod R. The point H is found as before, and then the length from centre to centre of link L is found, and with this radius and from H as a centre the arc P is drawn, and where P intersects the centre line J of R is the new position for the eye or centre Q of R.

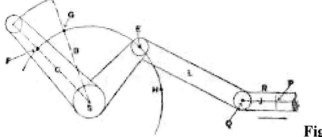

Fig. 261.

In Figure 262 we have a case of a similar lever actuating a plunger in a vertical line, it being required to find how much a given amount of motion of the long arm will actuate the plunger. Suppose the long arm to move to A, then draw the lines B C and the circle D. Take the radius or distance F, G, and from E mark on D the arc H. Mark the centre line J of the rod. Now take the length from E to I of the link, and from H as a centre mark arc K, and at the intersection of K with J is where the eye I will be when the long arm has moved to A.

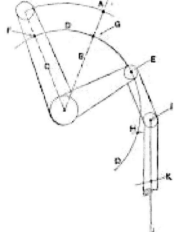

Fig. 262.

In Figure 263 are two levers upon their axles or shafts S and S'; arm A is connected by a link to arm B, and arm C is connected direct to a rod R. It is required to find the position of centre G of the rod eye when D is in position E, and when it is also in position F. Now the points E and F are, of course, on an arc struck from the axis S, and it is obvious that in whatever position the centre H may be it will be somewhere on the arc I, I, which is struck from the centre S'. Now suppose that D moves to E, and if we take the radius

D, H, and from E mark it upon the arc I as at V, then H will obviously be the new position of H. To find the new position of G we first strike the arc J, J, because in every position of G it will be somewhere on the arc J, J. To find where that will be when H is at V, take the radius H, G, and from V as a centre mark it on J, J, as at K, which is the position of G when D is at E and H is at V. For the positions when D is at F we repeat the process, taking the radius D, H, and from F marking P, and with the radius H, G, and from P as a centre marking Q; then P is the new position for H, and Q is that for G.

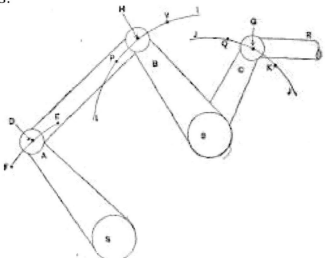

Fig. 263.

In Figure 264 a lever arm A and cam C are in one piece on a shaft. S is a shoe sliding on the line *x*, and held against the cam face by the rod R; it is required to find the position of the face of the shoe against the cam when the end of the arm is at D.

Draw line E from D to the axis of the shaft and line F. From the shaft axis as a centre draw circle W; draw line J parallel to *x*. Take the radius G H, and from K as a centre mark point P on W; draw line Q from the shaft axis through P, and mark point T. From the shaft axis as a centre draw from T an arc, cutting J at V, and V is the point where the face of the shoe and the face of the cam will touch when the arm stands at D.

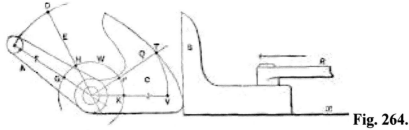

Fig. 264.

Let it be required to find the amount of motion imparted in a straight line to a rod attached to an eccentric strap, and the following construction may be used. In Figure 265 let A represent the centre of the shaft, and, therefore, the axis about which the eccentric revolves. Let B represent the centre of the eccentric, and let it be required to find in what position on the line of motion x, the centre C of the rod eye will be when the centre B of the eccentric has moved to E. Now since A is the axis, the centre B of the eccentric must rotate about it as denoted by the circle D, and all that is necessary to find the position of C for any position of eccentric is to mark the position of B on circle D, as at E, and from that position, as from E, as a centre, and with the length of the rod as a radius, mark the new position of C on the line x of its motion. With the centre of the eccentric at B, the line Q, representing the faces of the straps, will stand at a right angle to the line of motion, and the length of the rod is from B to C; when the eccentric centre moves to E, the centre line of the rod will be moved to position P, the line Q will have assumed position R, and point C will have moved from its position in the drawing to G on line x. If the eccentric centre be supposed to move on to F, the point C will move to H, the radii B C, E G, and F H all being equal in length. Now when the eccentric centre is at E it will have moved one-quarter of a revolution, and yet the point C will only have moved to G, which is not central between C and H, as is denoted by the dotted half circle I.

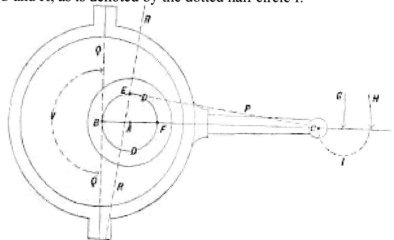

Fig.

265.

On the other hand, while the eccentric centre is moving from E to F, which is but one-quarter of a revolution, the rod end will move from G to H. This occurs because the rod not only moves *endwise*, but the end connected to the eccentric strap moves towards and away from the line *x*. This is shown in the figure, the rod centre line being marked in full line from B to *x*. And when B has moved to E, the rod centre line is marked by dotted line E, so that it has moved away from the line of motion B *x*. In Figure 266 the eccentric centre is shown to stand at an angle of 45 degrees from line *q*, which is at a right angle to the line of motion *x x*, and the position of the rod end is shown at C, J and H representing the extremes of motion, and G the centre of the motion.

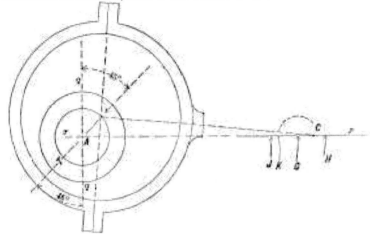

Fig. 266.

If now we suppose the eccentric centre to stand at T, which is also an angle of 45 degrees to *q*, then the rod end will stand at K, which is further away from G than C is; hence we find that on account of the movement of the rod out of the straight end motion, the motion of the rod end becomes irregular in proportion to that of the eccentric, whose action in moving the eye C of the rod in a straight line is increased (by the rod) while it is moving through the half rotation denoted by V in figure, and diminished during the other half rotation.

In many cases, as, for example, on the river steamboats in the Western and Southern States, cams are employed instead of eccentrics, and the principles involved in drawing or marking out such cams are given in the following remarks, which contain the substance of a paper read by Lewis Johnson before the American Society of Mechanical Engineers. In Figure 267 is a side view of a pair of cams; one, C, being a full stroke cam for operating the valve that admits steam to the engine cylinder; and the other, D, being a cam to cut off the steam supply at the required point in the engine stroke. The positions of these cams with relation to the position of the crank-pin need not be commented upon here, more than to remark that obviously the cam C must operate to open the steam inlet valve in advance of cam D, which operates to close it and cause the steam to act expansively in the cylinder, and that the angle of the throw line of the cut-off valve D to the other cam or to the crank-pin varies according as it is required to cut off the steam either earlier or later in the stroke.

The cam yoke is composed of two halves, Y and Y', bolted together by bolts B, which have a collar at one end and two nuts at the other end, the inner nuts N N enabling the letting together of the two halves

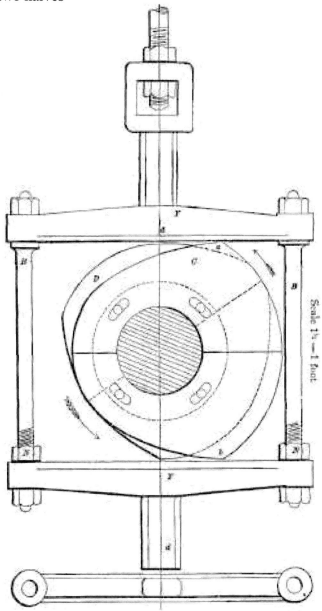

Fig. 267.

of the yoke to take up the wear. It is obvious that as the shaft revolves and carries the cam with it, it will, by reason of its shape, move the yoke back and forth; thus, in the position of the parts shown in Figure 267, the direction of rotation being denoted by the arrow, cam C will, as it rotates, move the yoke to the left, and this motion will occur from the time corner *a* of the cam meets the face of Y' until corner *b* has passed the centre line *d*. Now since that part of the circumference lying between points *a* and *b* of the cam is an arc of a circle, of which the axis of the shaft is the centre, the yoke will remain at rest until such time as *b* has passed line *d* and corner *a* meets the jaw Y of the yoke; hence the period of rest is determined by the amount of circumference that is made concentric to the shaft; or, in other words, is determined by the distance between *a* and *b*.

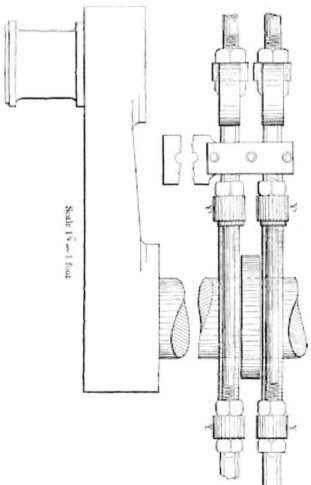

Fig. 268.

The object of using a cam instead of an eccentric is to enable the opening of the valves abruptly at the beginning of the piston stroke, maintaining a uniform steam-port opening during nearly the entire length of stroke, and as abruptly closing the valves at the termination of the stroke.

Figure 268 is a top view of the mechanism in Figure 267; and Figure 269 shows an end view of the yoke. At B, in Figure 268, is shown a guide through which the yoke-stem passes so as to be guided to move in a straight line, there being a guide of this kind on each side of the yoke.

The two cams are bolted to a collar that is secured to the crank-shaft, and are made in halves, as shown in the figures and also in Figures 270 and 271, which represent cams removed from the other mechanism. To enable a certain amount of adjustment of the cams upon the collar, the bolts which hold them to the collar fit closely in the holes in the collar, but the cams are provided with oblong bolt holes as shown, so that the position of either cam, either with relation to the other cam or with relation to the crank-pin, can be adjusted to the extent permitted by the length of the oblong holes.

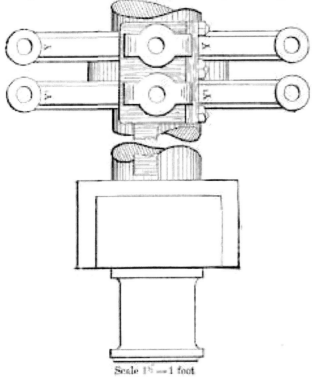

Scale 1" = 1 foot

Fig. 269.

The crank is assumed in the figures to be on its dead centre nearest to the engine cylinder, and to revolve in the direction of the arrows. The cams are so arranged that their plain unflanged surfaces bolt against the collar.

The method of drawing or marking out a full stroke cam, such as C in Figure 267, is illustrated in Figure 272, in which the dimensions are assumed to be as follows:

Diameter of crank shaft, 7-1/2 inches; travel of cam, 3 inches; width of yoke, 18 inches.

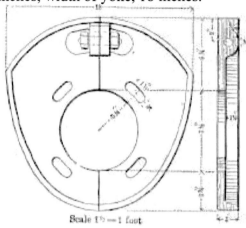

Scale 1½ — 1 foot

Fig. 270.

The circumference of the cam is composed of four curved lines, P, P', K 1, and K 2. The position of the centre of the crank shaft in this irregularly curved body is at X. The arcs K 1 and K 2 differ in radius, but are drawn from the same point, X, and hence are concentric with the crank shaft.

The arcs P, P', are of like radius, but are drawn from the opposite points S, S', shown at the intersection of the arcs P, P', with the arc K 1. Thus arcs P, P', are eccentric to the crank shaft.

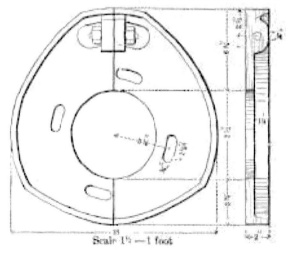

Scale 1½ — 1 foot

Fig. 271.

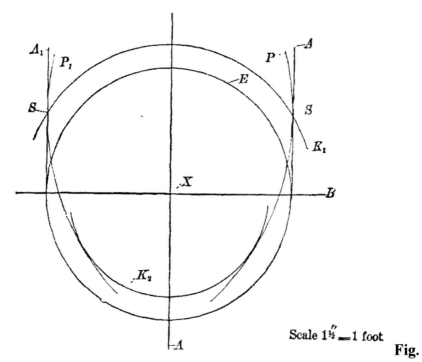

Scale $1\tfrac{1}{2}'' = 1$ foot

Fig. 272.

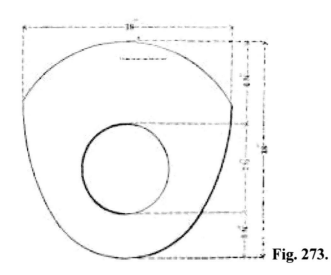

Fig. 273.

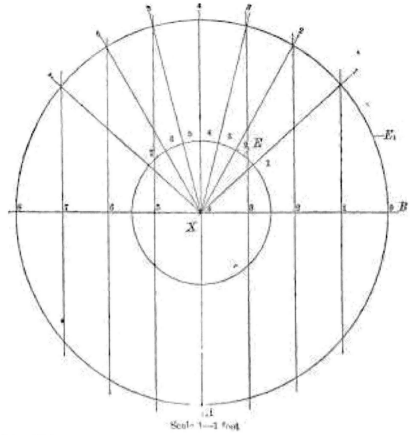

Fig. 274.

To draw the cam place one point of the dividers at X, which is the centre of the crank shaft, and draw the circle E equal to width of yoke, 18 inches. Through this centre X, draw the two right lines A and B. On the line B, at the intersection of the curved line E, draw the two vertical lines A 1, A 1. With a radius of 10-1/2 inches, and with one point of the dividers at X, draw the arc K 1. With a radius of 7-1/2 inches, and one point of the dividers at X, draw the arc K 2. With a radius of 18 inches, and one point of the dividers at the intersection of the arc E, with the vertical line A 1 at S, draw the arc P opposite to S, and let it merge or lose itself in the curved line K 2. Draw the other curved line P' from the other point S, and we have a full stroke cam of the dimensions required, and which is represented in Figure 273, removed from the lines used in constructing it.

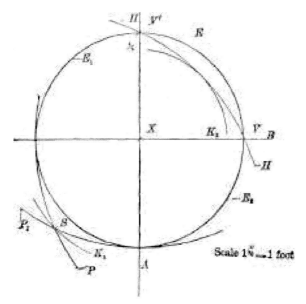

Fig. 275.

The engravings from and including Figure 274 illustrate the lines embracing cut-off cams of varying limits of cut-off, but all of like travel and dimensions, which are the same as those given for the full stroke cam in Figure 272.

In drawing cut-off cams, the stroke of the engine plays a part in determining their conformation, and in the examples shown this is assumed to be 4 feet. Figure 274 illustrates the manner of finding essential points in drawing or marking out cut-off cams. With X as a centre, and a radius of 2 feet, draw the circle E 1, showing the path of the crank-pin in making a revolution. This circle has a diameter of 4 feet, equal to the stroke of the engine. Draw the horizontal line B, passing through the centre of circle E 1. Within the limits of circle E 1, subdivide line B into eight equal parts, as at 1, 2, 3, 4, etc. Draw the vertical lines, 1, 2, 3, 4, etc., until they each intersect the circle E 1.

With X as a centre, draw the circle E, having a diameter of 18 inches, equal to the space in the yoke embracing the cam.

From the centre X draw the series of radial lines through the points of intersection of the vertical lines 1, 2, 3, 4, etc., from the circle E 1, and terminating at X. We will now proceed to utilize the scale afforded by Figure 274, in laying off the cut-off cam shown in Figure 276, of half stroke limit.

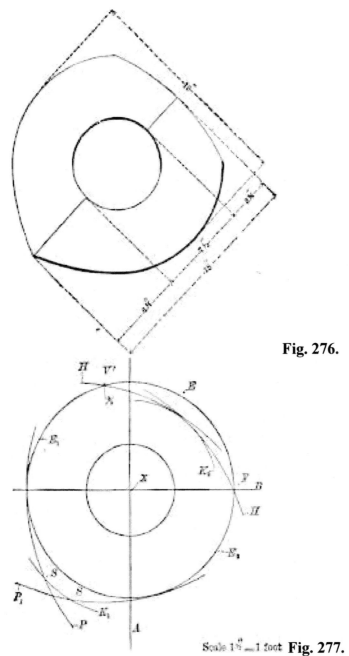

Fig. 276.

Fig. 277.

With X as a centre, draw the circle E, Figure 275, having a diameter of 18 inches. Bisect this circle with the straight lines A and B, which bear the same relation to their enclosing circle that the lines A, B, do to the circle E in Figure 274.

It will be observed, in Figure 274, that the vertical line A is (at the top half) also No. 4, representing 4/8, or half of the stroke. With a radius of 18 inches, and one point of the dividers placed at

V, which is at the intersection of the circle E with the horizontal line B in Figure 275, draw the arc P. With the same radius and with one compass point rested at V', draw the arc P'; then two arcs, P and P', intersecting at the point S.

With the same radius and one point of the compasses at S, draw the arc H H. The arcs K 1 and K 2 are drawn from the centre X, with a radius of 10-1/2 for K 1 and 7-1/2 inches for K 2, and only serve in a half stroke cam to intersect the curved lines already drawn, as shown in Figure 275. In practice, the sharp corner at S would be objectionable, owing to rapid wear at this point; and hence a modification of the dimensions for this half stroke cam would be required to obtain a larger wearing surface at the point S, but the cam of this limit (1/2 stroke) is correctly drawn by the process described with reference to Figure 275, the outline of the cam so constructed being shown in Figure 276.

In Figure 278 is shown a cam designed to cut off the steam at five-eighths of the piston stroke, the construction lines being given in Figure 277, for which draw circle E and straight lines A and B, as in the preceding example. By reference to Figure 274 it will be observed that the diagonal line drawn through circle E at 5 is drawn from the straight line marked 5, which intersects circle E 1, and as this straight line 5 represents five-eighths of the stroke laid off on line B, it determines the limit of cut-off on the five-eighths cam in Figure 277.

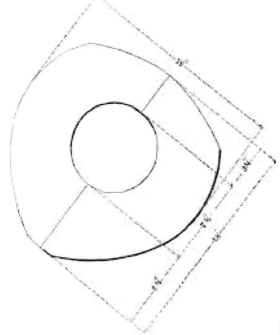

Fig. 278.

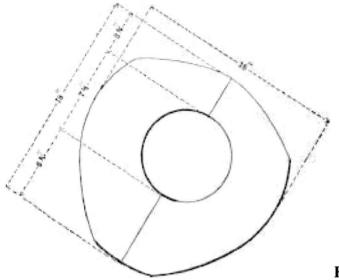

Fig. 279.

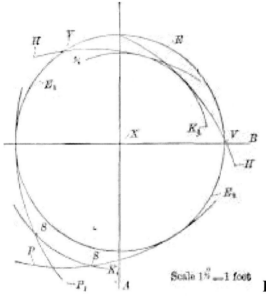

Scale 1⅝—1 foot

Fig. 280.

Turning then to Figure 274, take on circle E the radius from radial line 4 to radial line 5, and mark it in Figure 277 from the vertical line producing V'.

Now, with a radius of 18 inches, and one point of the dividers fixed at point V, forming the intersection of the circle E with the horizontal line B, draw the arc P. With the same radius, and one point of the dividers fixed at point V', draw the opposite arc P'.

With a radius of 10-1/2 inches from the centre X, draw the arc K 1, intersecting lines P P', at S S. With a radius of 7-1/2 inches, draw the curved line K 2, opposite to curved line K 1. Now, with a radius of 18 inches, and one point of the dividers fixed alternately at S S, draw the arcs H, H, from their intersection with the circle E, until they merge into the curved line K 2. These curved lines embrace a cut-off cam of five-eighths limit, shown complete in Figure 278.

From the instructions already given it should be easy to understand that the three-fourths and seven-eighths cams, shown in Figures 279, 280, 281 and 282, are drawn by taking the points of their cut-off from the same scale shown in Figure 274, at the diagonal points 6 and 7, intersecting circle E in that figure; and cut-off cams of intermediate limit of cut-off can be drawn by further subdividing the stroke line B, in Figure 274, into the required limits.

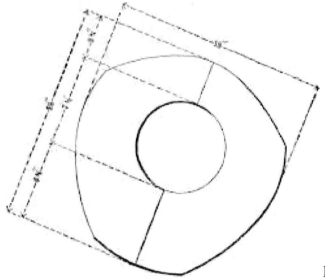

Fig. 281.

Cut-off cams of any limit are necessarily imperfect in their operations as to uniformity of cut-off from opposite ends of the slides, not from any defect in the rule for laying them off, but from the well-known fact of the crank pin travelling a greater distance, while driven by the piston from the centre of the cylinder, through its curved path from the cylinder, over its centre, and back to the centre of the cylinder, than in accomplishing the remaining distance of its path in making a complete revolution; and, although the subdivisions of eighths of the stroke line B, in Figure 274, does not truly represent a like division of the piston stroke, owing to deviation, caused by inclination of the connecting rod in traversing from the centres to half stroke, still it will be found that laying off a cut-off cam by this rule is more nearly correct than if the divisions on stroke line B were made to correspond exactly with a subdivision of piston stroke into eighths.

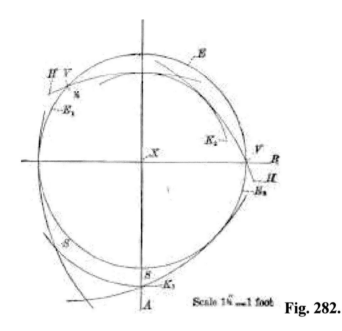

Scale 1⅛ = 1 foot   **Fig. 282.**

The cut-off in cams laid off by the rules herein described is greater in travelling from one side of the slides than in travelling from the opposite end, one cut-off being more than the actual cut-off of piston stroke, and the other less; and in practical use, owing to play or lost motion in the connections from cam to valve, the actual cut-off is less than the theoretical; hence cut-off cams are usually laid off to compensate for lost motion; that is, laid off with more limit; for instance, a five-eighths cam would be laid off to cut-off at eleven-sixteenths instead of five-eighths.

Figure 283 represents the motion a crank, C, imparts to a connecting rod, represented by the thick line R, whose end, B, is supposed to be guided to move in a straight line. The circle H represents the path of the crank-pin, and dots 1, 2, 3, etc., are 24 different crank-pin positions equidistant on the circle of crank-pin revolution.

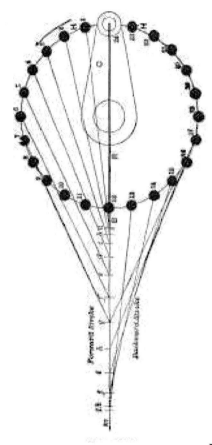

Fig. 283.

Suppose the crank-pin to have moved to position 1, and with the compasses set to the length of the rod R, we set one point on the centre of position 1, and mark on the line of motion *m* the line *a*, which will be the position rod end B will have moved to. Suppose next that the crank-pin has moved into position 2, and with the compass point on the centre of 2 we mark line 2, showing that while the crank-pin moved from 1 to 2, the rod end moved from *a* to *b*; by continuing this process we are enabled to discern the motion for the whole of the stroke. The backward stroke will be the same, for corresponding crank-pin positions, for both strokes; thus, when the rod end is at 7 the crank-pin may be at 7 or at 17. This fact enables us to find the positions for the positions later than 6, on the other side of the circle, as at 17, 16, 15, etc., which keeps the engraving clear.

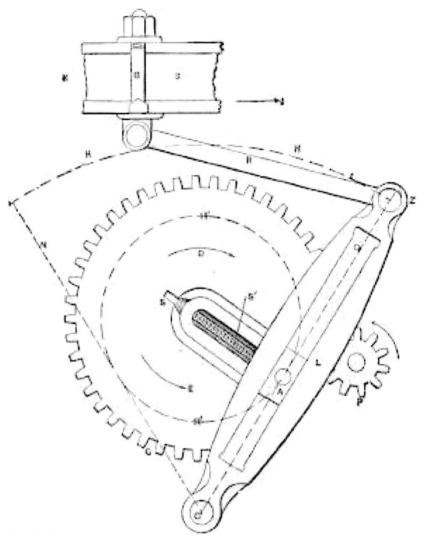

Fig. 284.

In Figure 284 a pinion, P, drives a gear-wheel, D, on which there is a pin driving the sliding die A in the link L, which is pivoted at C, and connected at its upper end to a rod, R, which is connected to a bolt, B, fast to a slide, S. It is required to find the motion of S, it moving in a straight line, dotted circle H' representing the path of the pin in the sliding die A, arc H representing the line of motion of the upper end of link L, and lines N, O, its centre line at the extreme ends of its vibrating motion. In Figure 285 the letters of reference refer to the same parts as those in Figure 284. We divide the circle H' of pin motion into 24 equidistant parts marked by dots, and through these we draw lines radiating from centre, C, and cutting arc H, obtaining on the arc H the various positions for end Z of rod R, these positions being marked respectively 1, 2, 3, 4, etc., up to 24. With a pair of compasses set to the length of rod R from 1 on H, as a centre, we mark on the line of motion of the slide, line *a*, which shows where the other end of rod R will be (or in other words, it shows the position of bolt B in Figure 284), when the centre of A, Figure 284, is in position 1, Figure 285.

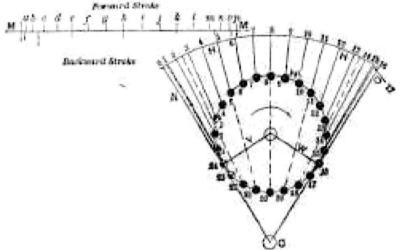

Fig. 285.

From 2 on arc H, we mark with the compasses line *b* on line M, showing that while the pin moved from 1 to 2, the rod R would move slide S, Figure 284, from *a* to *b*, in Figure 285. From 3 we mark *c*, and so on, all these marks being above the horizontal line M, representing the line of motion, and being for the forward stroke. For the backward stroke we draw the dotted line from position 17 up to arc H, and with the compasses at 17 mark a line beneath the line M of motion, pursuing the same course for all the other pin motions, as 18, 19, etc., until the pin arrives again at position 24, and the link at O, and has made a full revolution, and we shall have the motion of the forward stroke above and that of the backward one below the line of motion of the slide, and may compare the two.

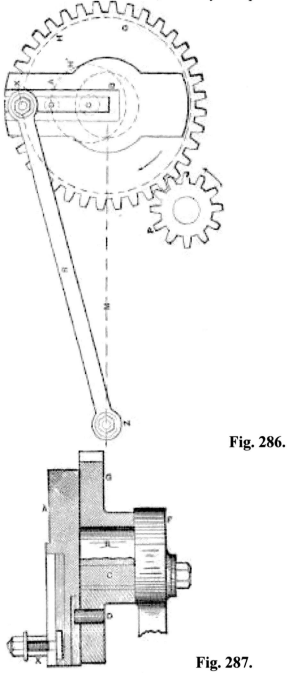

Fig. 286.

Fig. 287.

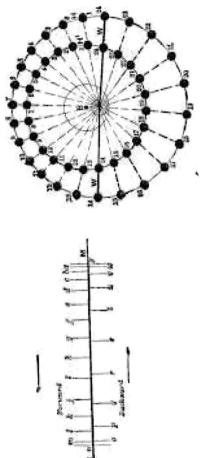

Fig. 288.

Figures 286 and 287 represent the Whitworth quick return motion that is employed in many machines. F represents a frame supporting a fixed journal, B, on which revolves a gear-wheel, G, operated by a pinion, P. At A is an arm having journal bearing in B at C. This arm is driven by a pin, D, fast in the gear, G; hence as the gear revolves, pin D moves A around on C as a centre of motion. A is provided with a slot carrying a pin, X, on which is pivoted the rod, R. The motion of end N of the rod R being in a straight line, M, it is required to find the positions of N during twenty-four periods in one revolution of G. In Figure 288 let H' represent the path of motion of the driving pin D, about the centre of B, and H the path of motion of X about the centre C; these two centres corresponding to the centres of B and C respectively, in Figure 287.

Fig. 289.

Let the line M correspond to the line of motion M in Figure 286. Now since it is the pin D, Figure 287, that drives, and since its speed of revolution is uniform, we divide its circle of motion H' into twenty-four equal divisions, and by drawing lines radiating from centre C, and passing through the lines of division on H' we get on circle H twenty-four positions for the pin X in Figure 286. Then setting the compasses to the length of the rod (R, Figure 286), we mark from position 1 on circle H as a centre line, *a*; from position 2 on H we mark line *b*, and so on for the whole twenty-four positions on circle H, obtaining from *a* to *n* for the forward, and from *n* to *y* for the motion during the backward stroke. Suppose now that the mechanism remaining precisely the same as before, the line M of motion be in a line with the centres C, B, instead of at a right angle to it, as it is in Figure 286, and the motion under this new condition will be as in Figure 289; the process for finding the amount of motion along M from the motion around H being precisely as before.

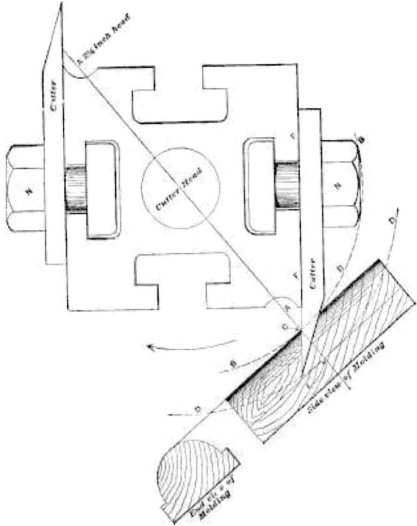

Fig. 290.

In Figure 290 is shown a cutter-head for a wood moulding machine, and it is required to find what shape the cutting edge of the cutter must be to form a moulding such as is shown in the end view of the moulding in the figure. Now the line A A being at a right angle to the line of motion of the moulding as it is passed beneath the revolving cutter, or, what is the same thing, at a right angle to the face of the table on which the moulding is moved, it is obvious that the highest point C of the moulding will be cut to shape by the point C of the cutter; and that since the line of motion of the end of the cutter is the arc D, the lowest part of the cutter action upon the moulding will be at point E. It will also be obvious that as the cutter edge passes, at each point, its length across the line A A, it forms the moulding to shape, while all the cutting action that occurs on either side of that line is serving simply to remove material. All that we have to consider, therefore, is the action on line A A.

It may be observed also that the highest point C of the cutter edge must not be less than 1/4 inch from the corner of the cutter head, which gives room for the nut N (that holds the cutter to the head) to pass over the top of the moulding in a 2-1/2 inch head. In proportion as the heads are made larger, however, less clearance is necessary for the nut, as is shown in Figure 291, the cutter edge extending to C, and therefore nearly up to the corner of the head. Its path of motion at C is shown by dotted arc B, which it will be observed amply clears the nut N. In practice, however, point C is not in any size of cutter-head placed nearer than 1/4 inch from corner X of the cutter-head.

To find the length of the cutter edge necessary to produce a given depth of moulding, we may draw a circle *i*, Figure 292, equal in diameter to the size of the cutter head to be used, and line A A. The highest point of cutting edge being at *e*, and the lowest at g, then circles *d* and *f* represent the line of motion of these two points; and if we mark the cutter in, the necessary length of cutting edge on the cutter is obviously from *a* to *b*.

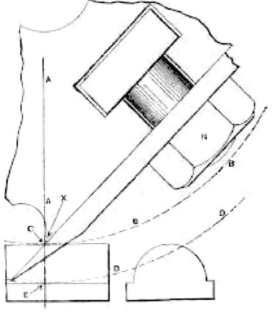

Fig. 291.

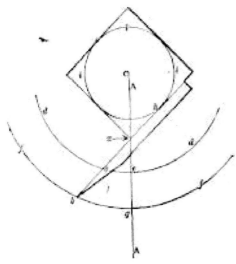

Fig. 292.

Now the necessary depth of cutter edge being found for any given moulding, or part of a moulding, the curves for the edge may be found as follows: Suppose the moulding is to be half round, as in the end view in Figure 290. The width of the cutter must of course equal the width of the moulding, and the length or depth of cutting edge required may be found from the construction shown in Figure 292; hence all that remains is to find the curve for the cutting edge. In Figure 293, let A A represent the centre of the cutter width, its sides being F F', and its end B B. From centre C draw circle D, the upper half of which will serve to represent the moulding. Mark on A the length or depth the cutting edge requires to be, ascertaining the same from the construction shown in Figure 292, and mark it as from C to K'. Then draw line E E, passing through point K. Draw line G, standing at the same angle to A A as the face *h b*, Figure 292, of the cutter does to the line A A, and draw line H H, parallel to G. From any point on G, as at I, with radius J, draw a quarter of a circle, as K. Mark off this quarter circle into equal points of division, as by 1, 2, 3, etc., and from these points of division draw lines, as *a*, *b*, *c*, etc.; and from these lines draw horizontal lines *d*, *e*, *f*, etc. Now divide the lower half of circle D into twice as many equal divisions as quarter circle K is divided into, and from these points of division draw perpendiculars *g*, *h*, *i*, etc. And where these perpendiculars cross the horizontal lines, as *d*, will be points through which the curve may be drawn, three of such points being marked by dots at *p*, *q*, *r*. If the student will, after having drawn the curve by this construction, draw it by the construction that was explained in connection with Figure 79, he will find the two methods give so nearly identical curves, that the latter and more simple method may be used without sensible error.

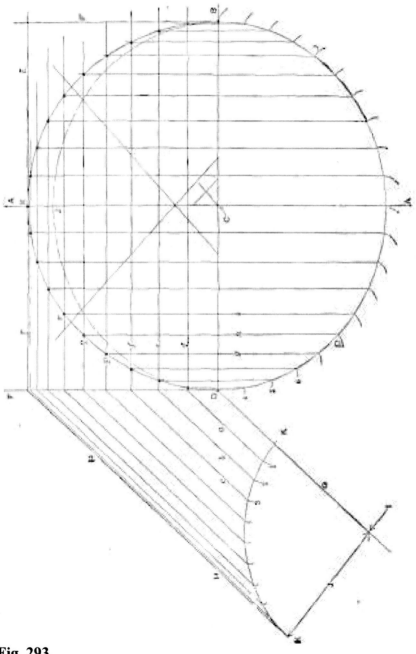

Fig. 293.

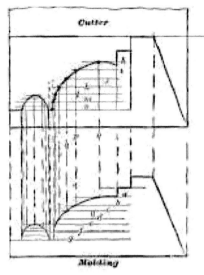

Fig. 294.

When the curves of the moulding are not arcs of circles they may be marked as follows:

Take the drawing of the moulding and divide each member or step of it by equidistant lines, as *a, b, c, d, e, f, g*, in Figure 294; above the moulding draw lines representing the cutter, and having found the depth of cutting edge for each member by the construction shown in Figure 292, finding a separate line, *a b*, for each member of the moulding, transfer the depths so found to the face of the cutter; divide the depth of each member of the cutter into as many equal divisions as the corresponding member of the moulding is divided into, as by lines *h, i, j, k, l, m, n*. Then draw vertical lines, as *o, p, q, r*, etc.; and where these lines meet the respective lines *h, i, j*, etc., are points in the curve, such points being marked on the cutter by dots.

CHAPTER XIII.

EXAMPLES IN LINE-SHADING AND DRAWINGS FOR LINE-SHADED ENGRAVINGS.

Although in workshop drawings, line-shading is rarely employed, yet where a design rather than the particular details of construction is to be shown, line-shading is a valuable accessory. Figure 295, for example, is intended to show an arrangement of idle pulleys to guide belts from one pulley to another; the principle being that so long as the belt passes to a pulley moving in line with the line of rotation of the pulley, the belt will run correctly, although it may leave the pulley at considerable angle. When a belt envelops two pulleys that are at a right angle to each other, two guide pulleys are needed in order that the belt may, in passing to each pulley, move in the same plane as the pulley rotates in, and the belt is in this case given what is termed a quarter twist.

It will be observed that by the line-shading even the twist of the belt is much more clearly shown than it would be if left unshaded.

An excellent example of shading is given in Figure 296, which is extracted from the *American Machinist*, and represents a cutting tool for a planing machine. The figure is from a wood engraving, but the effect may be produced by lines, the black parts being considered as simply broad black lines.

The drawings from which engravings are made are drawn to conform to the process by which the engraving is to be produced. Drawings that are shaded by plain lines may be engraved by three methods. First, the drawing may be photo-engraved, in which process the drawing is photographed on the metal, and every line appears in the engraving precisely as it appears in the drawing.

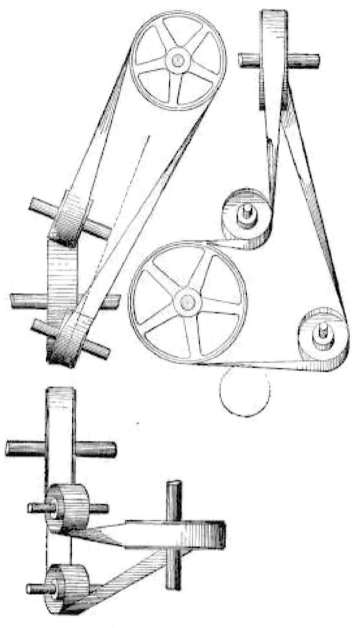

Fig. 295.

For this kind of engraving the drawing may be made of any convenient size that is larger than the size of engraving to be produced, the reduction of size being produced in the photographing process. Drawings for photo-engraving require to have the lines jet black, and it is to be remembered that if red centrelines are marked on the drawing, they will be produced as ordinary black lines in the engraving.

The shading on a drawing to be photo-engraved must be

produced by lines, and not by tints, for tints, whether of black or of colors, will not photo-engrave properly.

Fig. 296.

It is generally preferred to make the drawing for a photo-engraving larger than the engraving that is to be made from it, a good proportion being to make the drawing twice the length the engraving is to be. This serves to reduce the magnitude of any roughness in the lines of the drawing, and, therefore, to make the engraving better than the drawing.

The thickness of the lines in the drawing should be made to suit the amount of reduction to be made, because the lines are reduced in thickness in the same proportion as the engraving is reduced from the drawing. Thus the lines on an engraving reduced to one-half the dimensions of the drawing would be one-half as thick as the lines on the drawing.

Drawings for photo-engraving should be made on smooth-faced paper; as, for example, on Bristol board; and to make the lines clean and clear, the drawing instruments should be in the best of condition, and the paper or Bristol board quite dry. The India rubber should be used as little as possible on drawings to be photo-engraved, because, if used before the lines are inked in, it roughens the surface of the paper, and the inking lines will be less smooth and even at their edges; and for this reason it is better not to rub out any lines until all the lines have been inked in. If used to excess after the lines have been inked in it serves to reduce the blackness of the lines, and may so pale them that they will not properly photo-engrave.

To make a drawing for an engraver in wood it would be

drawn directly on the face of the box-wood block, on which it is to be engraved. The surface of the block is first whitened by a white water color, as Chinese white. If the drawing that is to be used as a copy is on sufficiently thin paper, its outline may be traced over by pencil lines, and the copy may then be laid face down on the wood block and its edges held to the block by wax, the pencilled lines being face to the block. The outline may then be again traced over with a pencil or pointed instrument, causing the imprint of the lead pencil lines to be left on the whitened surface of the block. If the copy is on paper too thick to be thus employed, a tracing may be made and used as above; it being borne in mind that the tracing must be laid with the pencilled lines on the block, because what is the right hand of the drawing on the block is the left hand in the print it gives. The shading on wood blocks is given by tints of India ink aided by pencilled lines, or of course pencilled lines only may for less artistic work be used. Another method is to photograph the drawing direct upon the surface of the wood block; it is unnecessary, however, to enter into this part of the subject.

The third method of producing an engraving from a drawing is by means of what is known as the wax process. Drawings for this process should be made on thin paper, for the following reasons: The process consists, briefly stated, in coating a copper plate with a layer of wax about 1/32 inch deep, and in drawing upon the wax the lines to compose the engraving, which lines are produced by means of tools that remove the wax down to the surface of the copper.

The plate and wax are then placed in a battery and a deposit of copper fills in the lines and surface of the wax, thus forming the engraving. Now if the drawing is made on thin paper, the engraver coats the surface of the drawing with a dry red pigment, and with a pointed instrument traces over the lines of the drawing, which causes them to leave a red imprint on the surface of the wax, and after the drawing is removed the engraver cuts these imprinted lines in the wax. If the drawing is on thick paper, this method of transferring the drawing to the wax cannot be used, and the engraver may take a tracing from the drawing and transfer from the tracing to the wax. It is obvious, also, that for wax engravings the drawing should be made of the same size that the engraving is required to be, or otherwise the tracing process described cannot be used. Figure 297 represents an engraving made by the wax process from a print from a wood engraving, and it is obvious that since all the lines drawn on the wax sink down to the surface of the copper plate, the shading is virtually composed of lines, the black surfaces being where the lines have been sufficiently close together and broad to remove all the wax enclosed within those surfaces.

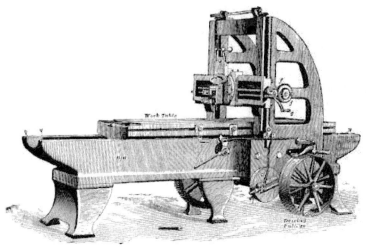

Fig. 297.

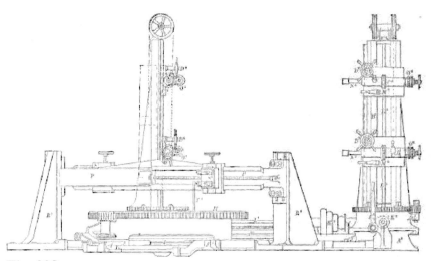

Fig. 298.

The wax process is, however, more suitable for engravings in plain outline only, and is especially excellent when the parts are small and the lines fall close together; as, for example, in Figures 298 and 299, which are engravings of a boiler drilling machine, and were produced for the *American Machinist* by tracing over a wood engraving from London, "Engineering" in the manner already described. The fineness and cleanness of the lines in the wax process is here well illustrated, the disposition of the parts being easily seen from the engraving, and easily followed in connection with the following description:

The machine consists of two horizontal bed-plates A 1 and A 2, made with V slides on top, and placed at right angles to each other. Upon each of the bed-plates is fitted a vertical arm B 1 and B 2, each of which carries two saddles, C 1 and C 2, these being each adjustable vertically on its respective arm by means of rack and pinion and hand wheels D 1 and D 2. The saddles are balanced so that the least possible exertion is sufficient to adjust them. The vertical arms, B 1 and B 2, are cast each with a round foot by which the arms are attached to the square boxes E 1 and E 2, which are fitted to the V slides on the horizontal beds A 1 and A 2, and are adjustable thereon by means of screw and ratchet motion F 1 and F 2. Each of the square boxes has cast on it a small arm G 1 and G 2, carrying studs upon which run pinions gearing into the circular racks at the foot of the vertical arms. The square boxes have each a circular groove turned in the top to receive the bolts by which the vertical arms are connected to them, and thus the vertical arms, and with them the drill spindles N 1 and N 2, are adjustable radially with the boiler—the adjustment being effected by means of the pinions and circular racks. The pinions are arranged so that they can be worked with the same screw key that is used for the bolts in the circular grooves.

The shell to be drilled is placed upon the circular table H, which is carried by suitable framework adjustable by means of screw on a V slide I, placed at an angle of 45° with the horizontal bed-plates. By this arrangement, when the table is moved along I, it will approach to or recede from all the drills equally. J 1 and J 2 are girders forming additional bearings for the framework of the table. The bed-plates and slides for the table are bolted and braced together, making the whole machine very firm and rigid. Power is applied to the machine through the cones K 1 and K 2, working the horizontal and vertical shafts L 1 and L 2, etc. On the vertical shafts are fitted coarse pitch worms sliding on feather keys, and carried with the saddles C 1 and C 2, etc. The worms gearing with the worm wheels M 1 and M 2 are fitted on the sleeves of the steel spindles N 1 and N 2. The spindles are fitted with self-acting motions O 1 and O 2, which are easily thrown in and out of gear.

The machine is also used for turning the edge of the flanges which some makers prefer to have on the end plates of marine boilers. The plates are very readily fixed to the circular table H, and the edge of the flange trued up much quicker than by the ordinary means of chipping. When the machine is used for this purpose, the cross beam P, which is removable, is fastened to the two upright brackets R 1 and R 2. The cross beam is cast with **V** slides at one side for a little more than half its length from one end, and on the opposite side for the same length, but from the opposite end. The **V** slides are each fitted with a tool box S 1 and S 2, having a screw adjustment for setting the tool to the depth of cut, and adjustable on the **V** slides of the cross beam to the diameter of the plate to be turned. This arrangement of the machine is also used for cutting out the furnace mouths in the boiler ends. The plate is fastened to the circular table, the centre of the hole to be cut out being placed over the centre of table; one or both of the tool boxes may be used. There is sufficient space between the upright brackets R 1 and R 2, to allow that section of a boiler end which contains the furnace mouths to revolve while the holes are being cut out; the plate belonging to the end of a boiler of the largest diameter that the machine will take in for drilling. The holes cut out will be from 2 feet 3 inches in diameter and upwards. Power for using the turntable is applied through the cone T. The bevel wheels, worms, worm wheels, and pinions for driving the tables are of cast steel, which is necessary for the rough work of turning the flanges.

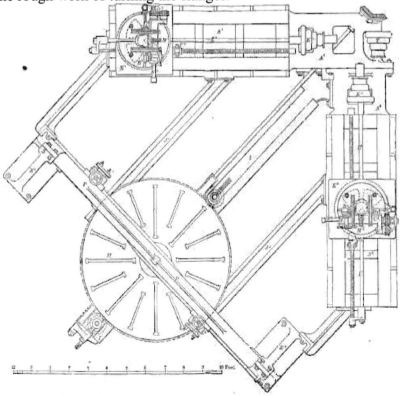

Fig. 299. (Page 275.)

As to the practical results of using the machine, the drills are driven at a speed of 340 feet per minute at the cutting edges. A jet of soapsuds plays on each drill from an orifice 1/32 in. in diameter, and at a pressure of 60 lbs. per square inch. A joint composed of two 1-inch plates, and having holes 1 and one-eighth in. in diameter, can be drilled in about 2-1/2 minutes, and allowing about half a minute for adjusting the drill, each drill will do about 20 holes per hour. The machine is designed to stand any amount of work that the drills will bear. The time required for putting on the end of a boiler and turning the flange thereon (say 14 feet diameter) is about 2-1/2 hours; much, however, depends on the state of the flanges, as sometimes they are very rough, while at others very little is necessary to true them up. The time required for putting on the plate containing the furnace mouths and cutting out three holes 2 feet 6 in. in diameter, the plate being 1 and one-eighth in. thick, is three hours. Of course, if several boilers of one size are being made at the same time, the holes in two or more of these plates can be cut out at once. The machine is of such design that it can be placed with one of the horizontal bed-plates (say A 1), parallel and close up to a wall of the boiler shop; and when the turning apparatus is being used, the vertical arm B 2 can be swiveled half way round on its square box E 2, and used for drilling and tapping the stay holes in marine boiler ends after they are put together; of course sufficient room must be left between bed-plate A 2, and the wall of boiler shop parallel with it, to allow for reception of the boiler to be operated upon.

It would obviously be quite difficult to draw such drawings as in Figures 298 and 299 on thin paper, so as to enable the drawing to be traced on the wax direct by the process before described, unless indeed the draftsman had considerable experience in fine work; hence, it is not uncommon to make the drawing large, and on ordinary drawing paper. The engraver then has the drawing photographed on the surface of the wax, and works to the photograph. The letters of reference in wax engravings are put in by impressing type in the wax, and in this connection it may be remarked that the letters I and O should not be used on drawings to be engraved by the wax process, unless they are situated outside the outlines of the drawing, because the I looks so much like part of a dotted line that it is often indistinguishable therefrom, while the O looks like a circle or an ellipse.

CHAPTER XIV.

SHADING AND COLORING DRAWINGS.

The shading or coloring of drawings by tints is more employed in large drawings than in small ones, and in Europe than in the United States; while on the other hand tinting by means of line-shading is more employed in the United States than in Europe, and more on small drawings than on large ones.

Many draftsmen adopt the plan of coloring the journals of shafts, etc., with a light tint, giving them the deepest tint at the circumference to give them a cylindrical appearance. This makes the drawing much clearer and takes but little time to do, and is especially advantageous where the parts are small or on a small scale, so that the lines are comparatively close together.

For simple shading purposes black tints of various degrees of darkness may be employed, but it is usual to tint brass work with yellow. Cast iron with India ink, wrought iron with Prussian blue, steel with as light purple tint produced by mixing India ink, Prussian blue and a tinge of crimson lake. Copper is tinted red. On plane surfaces an even tint of color is laid, but if the surfaces are cylindrical they are usually colored deeper at and near the circumference, and are tinted over the colors with light tints of India ink to show their cylindrical form.

If a drawing is to be colored or shaded with India ink the paper should be glued all around its edges to the drawing board, and then dampened evenly all over with a sponge, which will cause the paper to shrink and lay close to the surface of the drawing board. If, in applying a color or a tint, the color dries before the whole surface is colored, the color will not be of an equal shade; hence it is necessary before applying the color to dampen the surface, if it is a large one, so that the color at one part shall not get dry before there has been time to go over the whole surface; a more even depth of color is attained by the application of several coats of a light tint, than with one coat, giving the full depth of color. But if the paper is not allowed to dry sufficiently between the coats, or if it has been made too wet previous to the application of the colors, it will run in places, leaving other hollows into which the color will flow, making darker-colored spots. To avoid this the paper may be dried somewhat by the application of clean blotting paper.

To maintain an even shade of color, it is necessary to slightly stir up the color each time the brush is dipped into the color saucer or palette, especially when the coloring is composed of mixed colors, because the coloring matter is apt to separate from the water and sink to the bottom.

So, also, in mixing colors it is best to apply the end of the color to the surface of the palette and not to apply the brush direct to the cake of color, because the color is more completely mixed by contact with the palette than it can be by the brush, which may retain a speck of color that will, unless washed out, make a streak upon the drawing.

To graduate the depth of tint for a cylindrical surface, it is best to mix several, as, say three depths or degrees of tint, and to first use the darkest, applying it in the direction in which the piece is to be shaded darkest. The width this dark application should be is obviously determined by the diameter of the piece. The next operation is to lighten or draw the part, line or streak thus dark colored, causing it to get paler and paler as it approaches the axial line of the piece or cylinder. This lightening is accomplished as follows: The dark streak is applied along such a length of the piece that it will not dry before there has been time to draw it out or lighten it on the side towards the axis. A separate brush may then be wetted and drawn along the edge of the dark streak in short strokes, causing the color to run outwards and become lighter as it approaches the axis. It will be found that during this process the brush will occasionally require washing in water, because from continuous contact with the dark streak the tint it contains will darken. When the first coat has been laid and spread or drawn out from end to end of the piece, the process may be repeated two or three times, the most even results being obtained by making the first dark streak not too dark, and going over the drawing several times, but allowing the paper to get very nearly dry between each coat. In small cylindrical bodies, as, say 1/4 inch in diameter, the darkest line of shadow may be located at the lines representing the diameter of the piece, but in pieces of larger diameter the darkest line may be located at a short distance from the line that denotes the diameter or perimeter on the shadow or right-hand side of the piece, as is shown in many of the engravings that follow. It is obvious that if a drawing is to have dimensions marked on it, the coloring or tinting should not be deep enough to make it difficult to see the dimension figures.

The size of the brush to be used depends, of course, upon the size of the piece to be shaded or colored, and it is best to keep one brush for the dark tint and to never let the brush dry with the tint in it, as this makes it harsh. In a good brush the hairs are fine, lie close together when moistened, are smooth and yet sufficiently stiff or elastic to bend back slightly when the pressure is removed. If, when under pressure and nearly dry, the hairs will separate or the brush has no elasticity in it, good results cannot be obtained. All brushes should be well dried after use.

The light in shading is supposed to come in at the left-hand corner of the drawing, as was explained with reference to the shade line.

Excellent examples to copy and shade with the brush are given as follows:

Figure 300 represents a Medart pulley, constructed by the Hartford Steam Engineering Company; the arms and hub are cast in one piece, and the rim is a wrought iron band riveted to the arms, whose ends are turned or ground true with the hub bore. The figure is obviously a wood engraving, but it presents the varying degrees of shade or shadow with sufficient accuracy to form a good example to copy and brush shade with India ink. Figure 301 represents a similar pulley with a double set of arms, forming an excellent example in perspective drawing, as well as for brush-shading.

Fig. 300.

In brush-shading as with line-shading, the difficulties increase with an increase in the size of the piece, and the learner will find that after he has succeeded tolerably well in shading these small pulleys, it will be quite difficult, but excellent practice to shade the large pulley in Figure 302.

One of the principal considerations is to not let the color dry at the edges in one part while continuing the shading in another part of the same surface, hence it is best to begin at the edge or outline of the drawing and carry the work forward as quickly as possible, occasionally slightly wetting with water edges that require to be left while the shading is proceeding in another direction.

Fig. 301.

When it is required to show by the shading that the surfaces are highly polished, the lighter parts of the shading are made to contain what may be termed splashes of lighter and darker shadow, as in Figure 303, which represents an oil cup, having a brass casing enclosing a glass cylinder, which appears through the openings in the brass shell.

Figure 304 represents an iron planing machine whose line-shading is so evenly effected that it affords an excellent example of shading. Its parts are similar to those shown in the iron planer in Figure 297, save that it carries two sliding heads, so as to enable the use, simultaneously, of two cutting tools.

Fig.

302.

A superior example in shading is shown in Figures 305 and 306, which represent a plan and a sectional view of the steam-cylinder of a Blake's patent direct-acting steam-pump. The construction of the parts is as follows: A is the steam-piston, H 1 and H are the cylinder steam-passages; M is the cylinder exhaust port.

Fig. 303.

Fig. 304. (Page 282.)

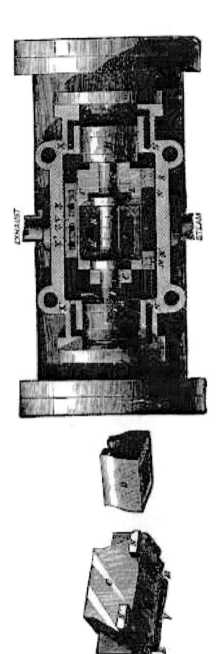

Fig. 305.

The main valve, whose movement alternately opens the ports for the admission of steam to, and the escape of steam from, the main cylinder, is divided into two parts, one of which, C, slides upon a seat on the main cylinder, and at the same time affords a seat for the other part, D, which slides upon the upper face of C. As shown in the engravings, D is at the left-hand end of its stroke, and C at the opposite or right-hand end of its stroke. Steam from the steam-chest, J, is therefore entering the right-hand end of the main cylinder through the ports E and H, and the exhaust is escaping through the ports H 1, E 1, K and M, which causes the main piston A to move from right to left. When this *piston* has nearly reached the left-hand end of its cylinder, the tappet arm, T, attached to the piston-rod, comes in contact with, and moves the valve rod collar O 1 and valve rod P, and thus causes C, together with the supplemental valves R and S S 1, which form, with C, *one casting*, to be moved from right to left. This movement causes steam to be admitted to the left-hand end of the supplemental cylinder, whereby its piston B will be forced towards the right, carrying D to the opposite or right-hand end of its stroke; for the movement of S closes N (the steam-port leading to the right-hand end), and the movement of S 1 opens N 1 (the steam-port leading to the opposite or left-hand end), at the same time the movement of V opens the right-hand end of this cylinder to the exhaust, through the exhaust ports X and Z. The parts C and D now have positions opposite to those shown in the engravings, and steam is therefore entering the main cylinder through the ports E 1 and H 1, and escaping through the ports H, E, K and M, which causes the main piston A to move in the opposite direction, or from left to right, and operations similar to those already described will follow, when the piston approaches the right-hand end of its cylinder. By this simple arrangement the pump is rendered positive in its action; that is, it will instantly start and continue working the moment steam is admitted to the steam-chest, while at the same time the piston is enabled to move as slowly as the nature of the duty may require. It will be noted that in Figure 305, the ports of C are shown through D, whose location is marked by dark shading. This obviously is not correct, because D being above C should be shaded lighter than C, and again the ports E 1 and K could not show dark through the port D. They might, of course, be shown by dotted outlines, but they would not appear to such advantage, and on this account it is permissible where artistic effect is sought, the object being to subserve the shading to making the mechanism and its operation clearly and readily understood.

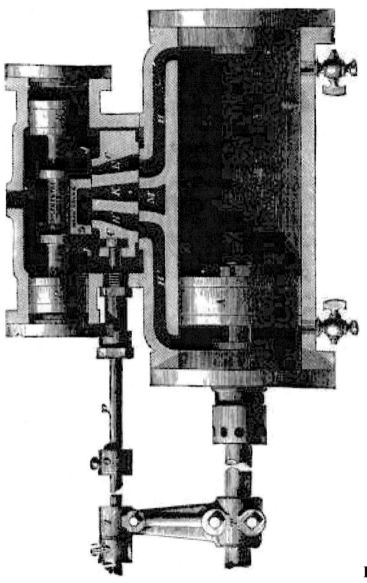

Fig. 306.

Figure 307 affords another excellent example for shading. It consists of an independent condenser, whose steam-cylinder and valve mechanism is the same as that described with reference to Figures 305 and 306.

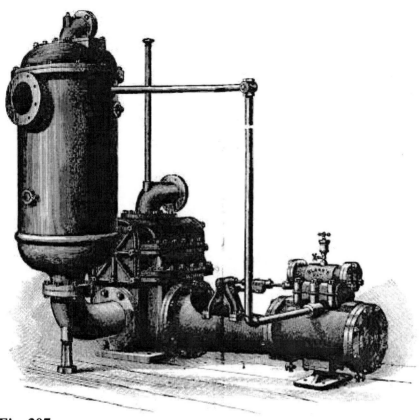

Fig. 307.

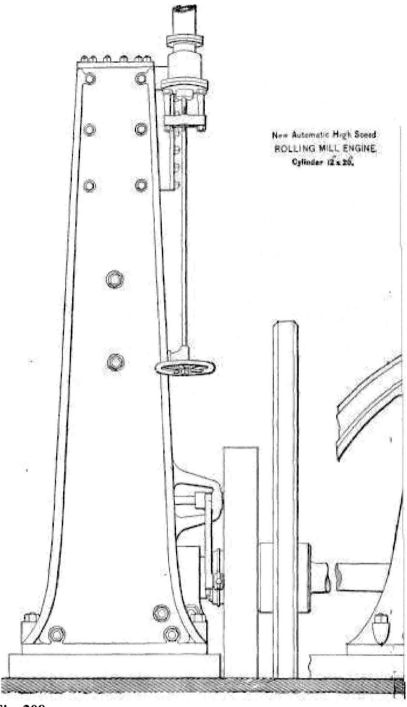

New Automatic High Speed
ROLLING MILL ENGINE
Cylinder 12˝ x 20˝.

Fig. 308.

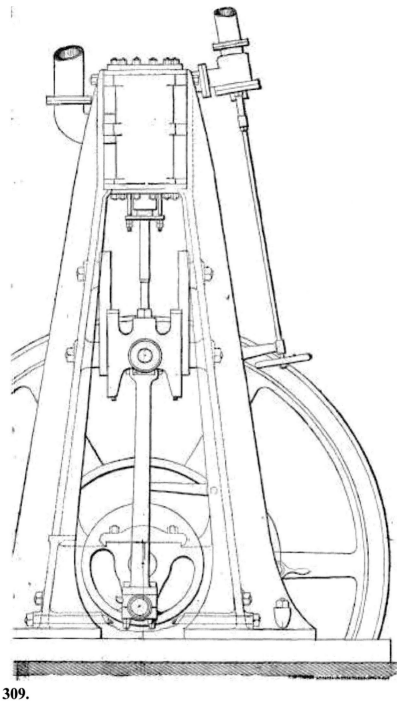

Fig. 309.

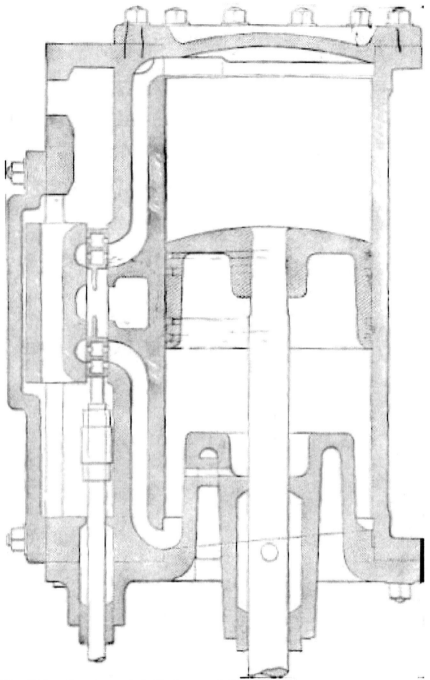

Fig. 310—Section of Cylinder and Steam Chest.

CHAPTER XV.

EXAMPLES IN ENGINE WORK.

In the figures from 308 to 328 inclusive are given three examples in engine work, all these drawings being from *The American Machinist*. Figures 308 to 314 represent drawings of an automatic high speed engine designed and made by Professor John E. and William A. Sweet, of Syracuse, New York. Figure 308 is a side and 309 an end view of the engine. Upon a bed-plate is bolted two straight frames, between which, at their upper ends, the cylinder is secured by bolts. The guides for the cross-head are bolted to the frame, which enables them to be readily removed to be replaned when necessary. The hand wheel and rod to the right are to operate the stop-cock for turning on and off the steam to the steam-chest.

The objects of the design are as follows: Figure 310 is a vertical section of the cylinder through the valve face, also showing the valve in section, and it will be seen that the lower steam passage enters the cylinder its full depth below the inside bottom, and that the whole inside bottom surface of the cylinder slopes or inclines towards the entrance of this passage. The object of this is to overcome the difficulty experienced from the accumulation of water in the cylinder, which, in the vertical engine, is usually a source of considerable annoyance and frequently the cause of accident.

Any water that may be present in the bottom finds its way by gravity to the port steam entrance, and is forced out by and with the exhaust steam at or before the commencement of the return stroke.

To assist in the escape of water from the top of the cylinder, the piston is made quite crowning at that end, the effect of which is to collect the water in a narrow band, instead of spreading it over a large surface. This materially assists in its escape, and at the same time presents a large surface for the distribution of any water that may not find its way out in advance of the piston.

The piston is a single casting unusually long and light, and is packed with four spring rings of 3/8 inch square brass wire.

The valve is a simple rectangular plate, working between the valve face and a cover plate, the cover plate being held in its proper position, relative to the back of the valve, by steam pressure against its outer surface, and by resting against loose distance pieces between its inner surface and the valve seat. This construction admits of the valve leaving the seat, if necessary, to relieve the cylinder from water, as in the instance of priming, and also, by the reduction of these pieces, admits of ready adjustment to contact, should it become necessary.

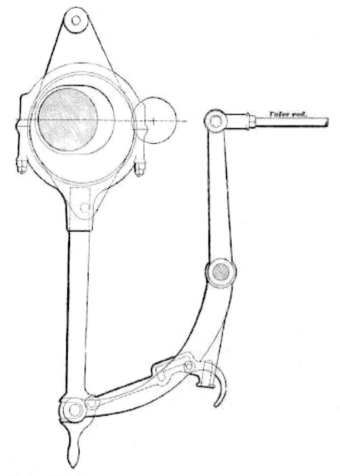

Fig. 311—

Valve Motion.

The cover plate is provided with recesses on its inner surface which exactly correspond with the ports in the valve face, and the corresponding ports and recesses are kept in communication with each other by means of relief passages in the valve. From this it will be seen that the valve is subjected to equal and balanced pressure on each of its sides, and hence, is in equilibrium.

The valve is operated through the valve motion, shown in Figure 311, the eccentric rod of which hooks on a slightly tapered block that turns on the pin of the rock arm, like an ordinary journal box.

The expansion, or cut-off, is automatically regulated by the operation of the governor in swinging the slotted eccentric in a manner substantially equivalent to moving it across the shaft, but is however favorably modified by the arrangement of the rock arm, which, in combination with the other motions, neutralizes the unfavorable operation of the usual shifting eccentric, and which, in connection with the large double port opening, provides for a good use of steam from 0 to 3/4 stroke.

The governor shown in Figure 312 is of the disc and single ball type, the centrifugal force of the ball being counteracted by a powerful spring. Friction is reduced to a minimum in the governor connection, by introducing steel rollers and hardened steel plates in such a manner as to provide rolling instead of sliding motion.

In order that a governor shall correctly perform its functions, it is unquestionably necessary that it have power largely in excess of the work required of it, and also that the friction shall represent a very low percentage of that power. In respect to this, especial means have been employed to reduce the friction; the valve being balanced, requires but little power to move it, while the governor ball being made heavy for the purpose of counterbalancing the weight of the eccentric and strap, its centrifugal force when the engine is at full speed is enormous, the spring to counteract it having to sustain from *two to three thousand pounds.* Under these circumstances, as might be expected, the regulation is remarkably good. This is a very important consideration in an engine working under the conditions of a roll-train engine.

Figure 313 represents a section of the pillow block box, crank-pin and wheel, together with the main journal. It will be seen that the end of the box next the crank wheel has a circular groove around its outside, and that a corresponding groove in the crank wheel projects over this groove. From this latter groove an oil hole of liberal size extends, as shown, to the surface of the crank-pin. Any oil placed at the upper part of the groove on the box finds its way by gravity into the groove in the crank wheel, and is carried by centrifugal force to the outside surface of the crank-pin; so that whatever other means of lubrication may be employed, this one will always be positive in its action. This cut also shows the manner in which the box overlaps the main journal and forms the oil reservoir.

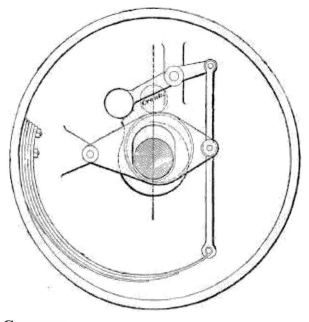

Fig. 312—Governor.

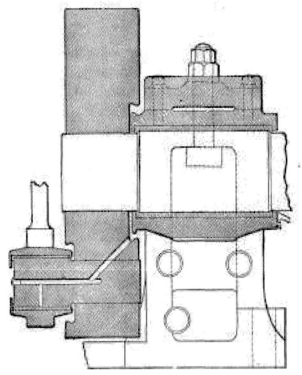

Fig. 313—Section of Pillow Block.

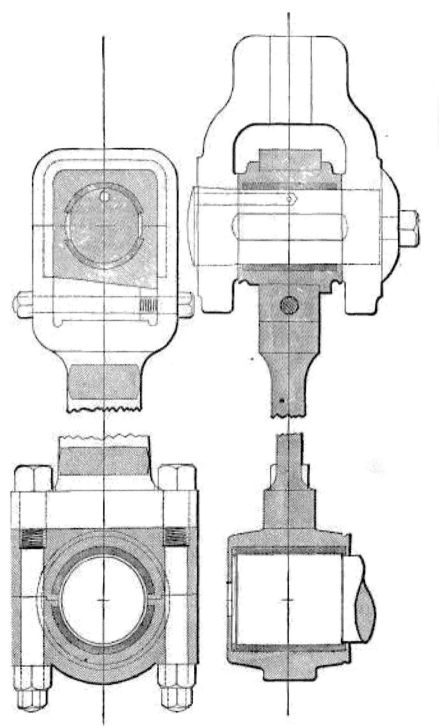

Fig. 314—Connecting Rod. (Page 295.)

Another feature in the construction of this box is the means by which it is made to adjust itself in line with the shaft. It will be observed that it rests on the bottom of the jaws of the frame on two inclined surfaces, which form equal angles with the axis of the shaft when in its normal position, and that by moving longitudinally in either direction, as may be necessary, the box will accommodate itself to a change in the alignment of the shaft. In order that it may be free to move for this purpose it is not fitted with the usual fore and aft flanges. By this means any slight derangement, as in either the outboard or inboard bearing wearing down the fastest, is taken care of, the movement of the box on the inclined surfaces being for this purpose equivalent to the operation of a ball and socket bearing.

Figure 314 gives a side and an edge view of the connecting rod, the rod being in section in the edge view, and the brasses in section lined in both views.

The cross-head pin, it will be observed, is tapered, and is drawn home in the cross-head by a bolt; the sides of the pin are flattened somewhat where the journal is, so that the pin may not wear oval, as it is apt to do, because of the pull and thrust strain of the rod brasses falling mainly upon the top and bottom of the journal, where the most wear therefore takes place. The brasses at the crossed end are set up by a wedge adjustable by means of the screw bolts shown. The cross-head wrist pin being removable from the cross-head enables the upper end of the rod to have a solid end, since it can be passed into place in the crossed and the wrist pin inserted through the two. The lower ends of the connecting-rod and the crank-pin possess a peculiar feature, inasmuch as by enlarging the diameter of the crank-pin, the ends of the brasses overlap, to a certain extent, the ends of the journal, thus holding the oil and affording increased lubrication. The segments that partly envelop the cross-head pin and crank-pin, and are section lined in two directions, producing crossing section lines, or small squares, show that the brasses are lined with babbitt metal, which is represented by this kind of cross-hatching. These drawings are sufficiently open and clear to form very good examples to copy and to trace on tracing paper.

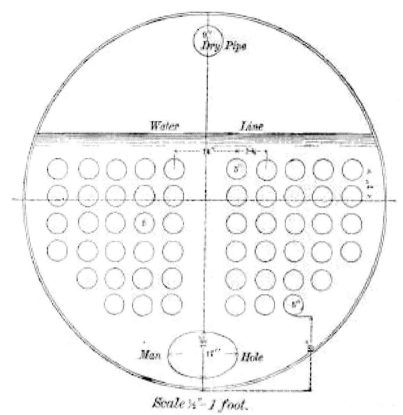

Fig. 315. (Page 296.)

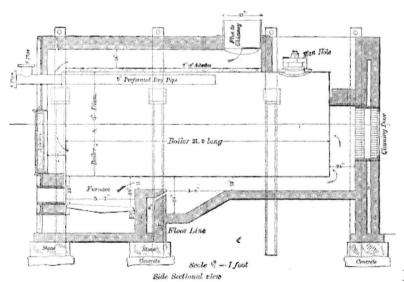

316.

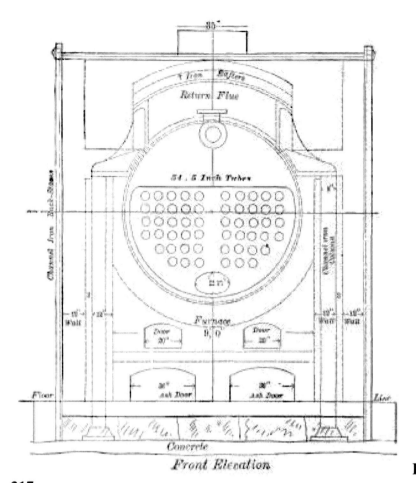

Front Elevation

Fig. 317.

Figures 315, 316 and 317 represent, in place upon its setting, a 200 horse-power horizontal steam-boiler for a stationary engine, and are the design of William H. Hoffman. The cross-sectional view of the boiler shell in Figure 315 shows the arrangement of the tubes, which, having clear or unobstructed passages between the vertical rows of tubes, permits the steam to rise freely and assists the circulation of the water. The dry pipe (which is also shown in Figure 316) is a perforated pipe through which the steam passes to the engine cylinder, its object being to carry off the steam as dry as possible; that is to say, without its carrying away with the steam any entrained water that may be held in suspension. Figure 316 is a side elevation with the setting shown in section, and Figure 317 is an end view of the boiler and setting at the furnace end. The boiler is supported on each side by channel iron columns, these being riveted to the boiler shell angle pieces which rest upon the columns. The heat and products of combustion pass from the furnace along the bottom of the boiler, and at the end pass into and through the tubes and thence over the top of the boiler to the chimney flue. There is shown in the bridge wall an opening, and its service is to admit air to the gases after they have passed the bridge wall, and thus complete the combustion of such gases as may have remained unconsumed in the furnace. The cleansing door at one end and that lined with asbestos at the other, are to admit the passage of the tube cleaners. The asbestos at the top of the boiler shell is to protect it from any undue rise in temperature, steam being a poorer conductor of heat than water, and it being obvious that if one side of the boiler is hotter than the other it expands more from the heat and becomes longer, causing the boiler to bend, which strains and weakens it. The sides of the setting are composed of a double row of brick walls with an air space of three inches between them, the object being to prevent as far as possible the radiation of heat from the walls. The brick-staves are simply stays to hold the brick work together and prevent its cracking, as it is apt, in the absence of staying, to do.

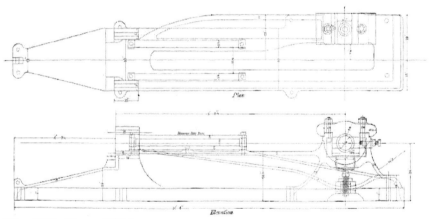

Fig. 318. (Page 299.)

Figures from 318 to 330 are working drawings of a 100-horse engine, designed also by William H. Hoffman.

Figure 318 represents a plan and a side view of the bed-plate with the main bearing and the guide bars in place. The cylinder is bolted at the stuffing box end to the bed-plate, and is supported at the outer end by an expansion link pivoted to the bed-plate. The main bearing is provided with a screw for adjusting the height of the bottom piece of the bearing, and thus taking up the wear. The guide bars are held to the bed in the middle as well as at each end.

Figures 319 and 320 represent cross sections of the bed-plate.

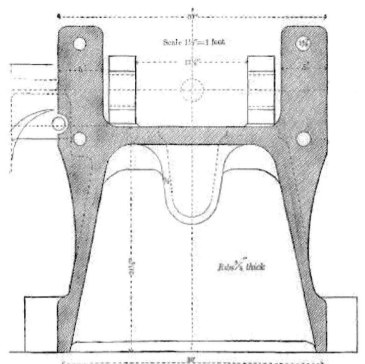

Fig.

319—Cross Section of Bed Plate near Junction with Cylinder. (Page 299.)

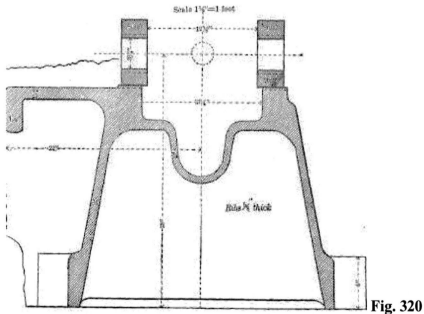

Fig. 320

Figure 321 represents a side elevation of the cylinder, and Figure 322 an end view of the same, the expansion support being for the purpose of permitting the cylinder to expand and contract under variations of temperature without acting to bend the bed-plate, while at the same time the cylinder is supported at both ends. The cylinder and cylinder covers are jacketted with live steam in the steam-spaces shown.

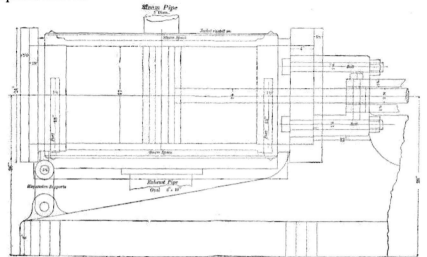

Fig. 321—100 H.P. Horizontal Steam-Engine—Elevation of Cylinder—Scale 1-1/2 " = 1 Foot. (Page 299.).

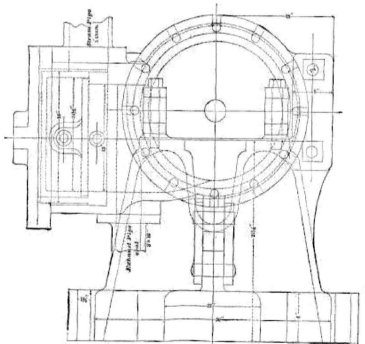

Fig. 322—100 H.P. Horizontal Steam-Engine—End View of Cylinder—Scale 1-1/2" = 1 Foot. (Page 299.)

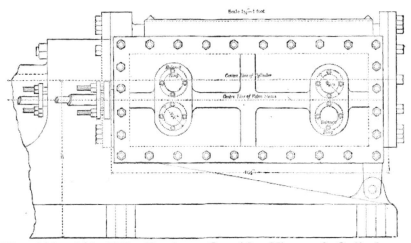

Fig. 323—100 H.P. Engine—Outside View of Cylinder and Steam-Chest. (Page 301.)

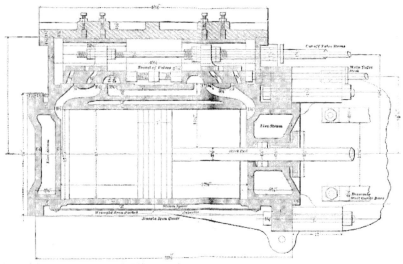

Fig. 324—Sectional View of Cylinder and Valves—Scale 1-1/2 Inches = 1 Foot. (Page 301.)

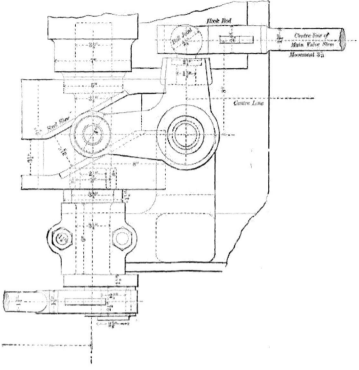

Fig.

325—Plan of Cut-off Device. (Page 301.)

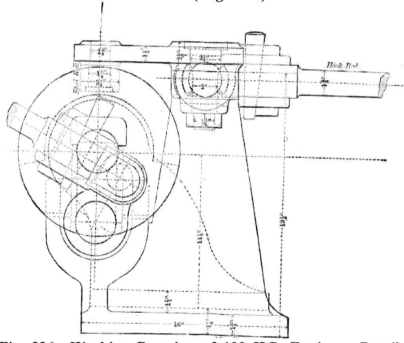

Fig. 326—Working Drawing of 100 H.P. Engine— Details of Main Valve Motion—Scale 3" = 1 Foot. (Page 301.)

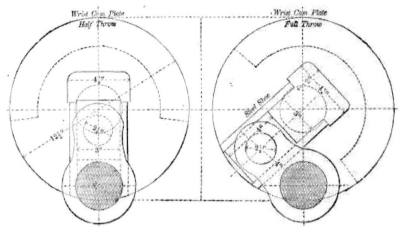

Fig. 327—Working Drawing of 100 H.P. Steam-Engine.—Wrist Plate.—3" = 1 Foot.

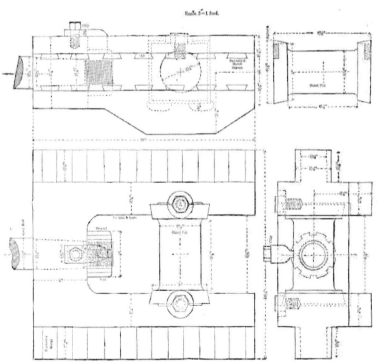

Fig. 328—100 H.P Horizontal Steam-Engine— Cross Head. (Page 301.)

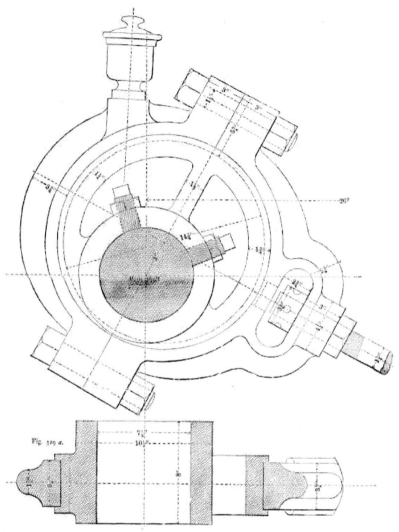

Fig. 329. Working Drawings of 100 H.P. Steam Engine— Eccentric and Eccentric Strap—Scale: 3" = 1 Foot. Page 301.)

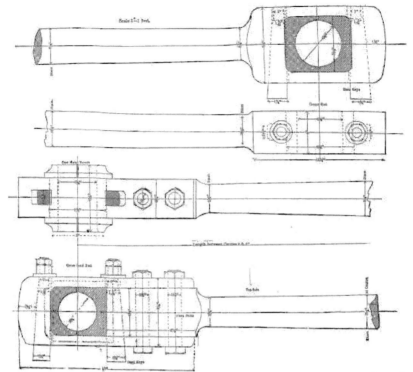

Fig. 330—100 H.P. Horizontal Steam-Engine—Connecting Rod. (Page 303.)

A view of the steam-chest side of the cylinder is given in Figure 323, and a horizontal cross section of the cylinder, the steam-chest and the valves, is shown in Figure 324. The main valves are connected by a right and left hand screw, to enable their adjustment, as are also the cut-off valves.

Figures 325 and 326 show the cam wrist plate and the cut-off mechanism. The cam wrist plate, which is of course vibrated by the eccentric rod, has an inclined groove, whose walls are protected from wear by steel shoes. In this groove is a steel roller upon a pin attached to the bell crank operating the main valve stem. The operation of the groove is to accelerate the motion imparted from the eccentric to the valve at one part of the latter's travel, and retard it at another, the accelerated portion being during the opening of the port for steam admission, and during its closure for cutting off, which enables the employment of a smaller steam-port than would otherwise be the case.

The shaft for the cam plate is carried in a bearing at one end, and fits in a socket at the other, the socket and bearing being upon a base plate that is bolted to the bed-plate of the engine; a side view of the construction being shown in Figure 327.

Figure 328 represents the cross-head, whose wrist pin is let into the cross-head cheeks, so that it may be removed to be turned up true. The clip is to prevent the piston rod nut from loosening back of itself.

Figure 329 represents a side view; and Figure 329 *a* a section through the centre of the eccentric and strap.

The eccentric is let into the strap and is provided with an eye to receive a circular nut by means of which the length of the eccentric rod may be adjusted, a hexagon nut being upon the other or outer end of the eye.

Figure 330 shows the construction of the connecting rod, the brasses of which are adjustable to take up the wear and to maintain them to correct length, notwithstanding the wear, by means of a key on each side of each pair of brasses, the keys being set up by nuts and secured by check nuts.

CPSIA information can be obtained at www.ICGtesting.com
Printed in the USA
LVOW10s1454190216

475864LV00017B/704/P